ALNMOUTH TO BERWICK

including the Seahouses and Tweed Dock branches

Roger Darsley & Dennis Lovett

Series editor Vic Mitchell

Front cover: The A3 class Pacific Flying Scotsman *and the train 'The Flying Scotsman' have always been associated with the East Coast Main Line (ECML). Here in 1968, in the early days of its preservation, no. 4472 is approaching Scremerston with an Up excursion train. It has two tenders, the second being an extra water carrier. Ironically, in a few miles it will pass over Lucker troughs. These will be removed at the official end of steam haulage. Thankfully main line steam haulage is still occasionally with us. (B.McCartney)*

Rear cover - upper: This is a postcard view, about 1920 of the Seahouses terminus of the North Sunderland Railway. Bamburgh *0-6-0ST Manning Wardle (1394 of 1898) is on the two-coach train for Chathill. (Northumberland Community/Armstrong Railway Photographic Trust ARPT)*

Back cover: Railway Clearing House map, dated 1947.

Readers of this book may be interested in the following societies:

Aln Valley Railway Trust
roger.jermy@alnvalleyrailway.co.uk

Friends of Berwick and District Museum and Archives
www.berwickfriends.org.uk

North Eastern Railway Association
membership@ner.org.uk

Railway Correspondence and Travel Society, NE Branch
rctsnewcastle@gmail.com

Published January 2021

ISBN 978 1 910356 50 0

Cover design Deborah Esher
Design Cassandra Morgan

Published by
Middleton Press
Easebourne Lane
Midhurst
West Sussex
GU29 9AZ
Tel: 01730 813169
Email: info@middletonpress.co.uk
www.middletonpress.co.uk

Printed and bound by CPI Group (UK) Ltd, Croydon, CR0 4YY

CONTENTS

14	Aln Valley Railway	29	Christon Bank	55	Lucker
1	Alnmouth for Alnwick	68	Crag Mill	52	Newham
16	Alnwick	34	Fallodon	44	North Sunderland
15	Alnwick Lionheart	81	Goswick	85	Scremerston
75	Beal	80	Holy Island	46	Seahouses
62	Belford	19	Lesbury	71	Smeafield
113	Berwick upon Tweed	25	Little Mill	99	Tweedmouth
37	Chathill	21	Longhoughton		

ACKNOWLEDGEMENTS

We are grateful for the assistance received from many of those mentioned in the photographic credits and to, G.Croughton, D.R.Dunn. R.Jermy, N. Langridge, A.P.McLean, D.W.Tyreman, J.P.Vickers, A.Wright, J.W.Yellowlees and A.E.Young.

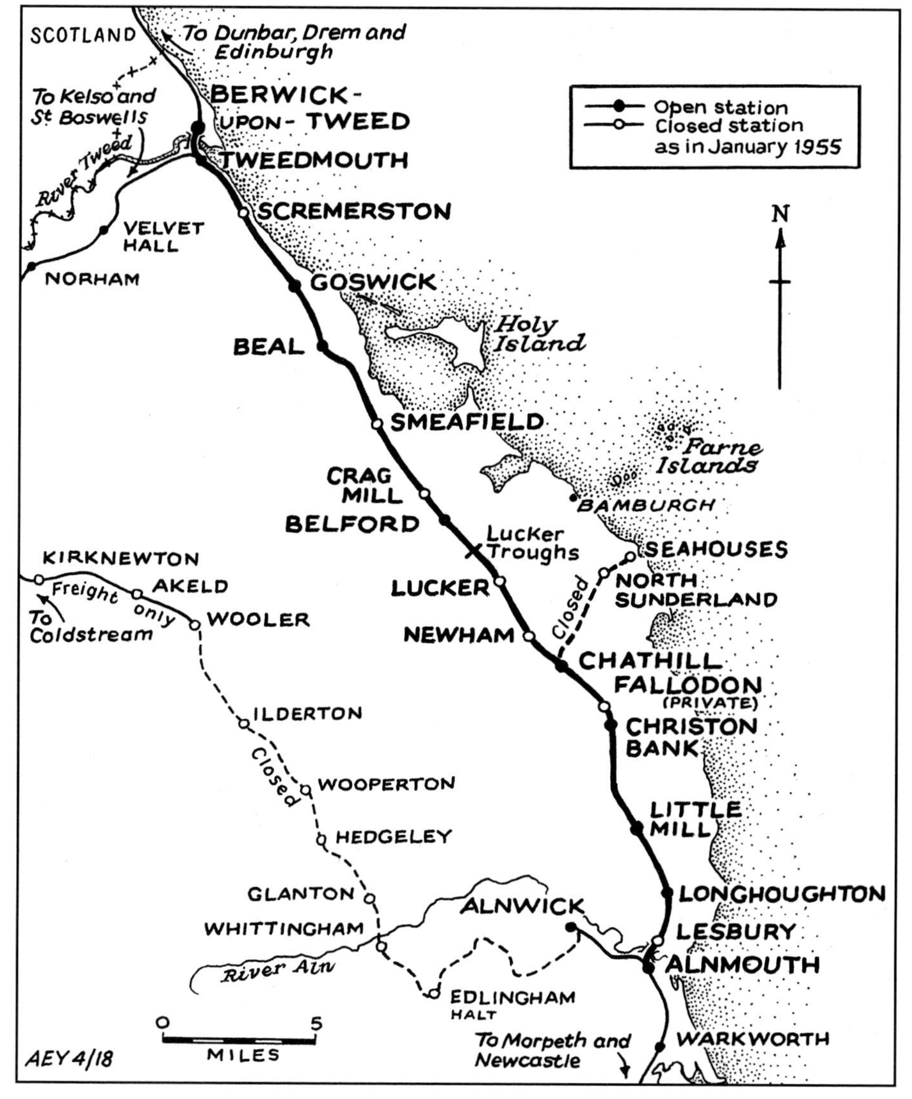

I. A map showing the East Coast Main Line between Alnmouth and Berwick along with the North Sunderland branch to Seahouses in 1955. (A.E.Young)

GEOGRAPHICAL SETTING

North Northumberland is an area which is rich in mineral outcrops. Coal mining took place at Scremerston near Berwick, whilst there were several quarries producing sandstone, whinstone and limestone some of which had their own industrial networks or were served by sidings from the main line. Forestry was another major industry.

The line runs close to the coast beyond Chathill, offering travellers stunning views of Holy Island or the beach at Spittal, Berwick's seaside resort. For an area with a proud maritime history, the railways served the harbours at Seahouses and at Tweed Dock, the latter proving both an engineering and operating challenge to serve it.

Today the area is also a mainly agricultural region whilst the tourist industry is a major employer.

Maps are derived from 25ins to 1 mile editions with North at the top unless otherwise stated.

HISTORICAL BACKGROUND

At the height of railway mania in the 1840s, much consideration was given to linking Newcastle to Berwick. Two main contenders emerged: the Newcastle & Berwick Railway and the Northumberland Railway, the latter proposing an atmospheric railway, already in use in Dublin and on the London & Croydon Railway and similar to the scheme that Brunel developed for the South Devon Railway between Exeter and Newton Abbot. This scheme did not prove popular with politicians and the Newcastle & Berwick Railway received its Act of Parliament on 31 July 1845.

1847 saw the Newcastle & Berwick amalgamate with the York & Newcastle to become the York, Newcastle & Berwick Railway. The new company would facilitate the building the Royal Border Bridge over the River Tweed (opened in 1850). At Berwick, the line shared station facilities with the North British Railway line from Edinburgh, which opened on the 22nd June 1846.

The line opened between Tweedmouth to Chathill on 29th March 1847 with the section between Morpeth and Chathill following on 1st July 1847. Several railway companies, including the YN&BR, merged on 31st July 1854 to become the North Eastern Railway (NER), which continued to operate services until the Grouping on 1st January 1923.

The North British Railway also became part of the London & North Eastern Railway (LNER) in 1923 and it was during the LNER period that faster and more powerful locomotives dominated the main line express services, whilst branch and local services also saw the introduction of newer locomotives and rolling stock.

Nationalisation followed in 1948 and it was not until the introduction of the powerful Deltic (later Class 55) locomotives in 1961 that services could be speeded up. It was during the 1950s that a number of local stations between Alnmouth and Berwick were closed.

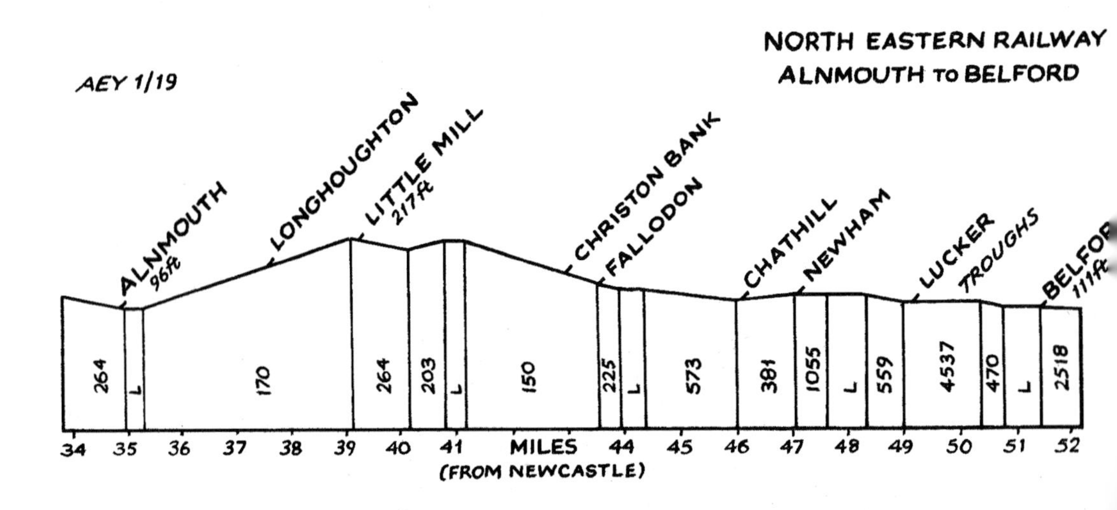

Journey time reductions on trains between London and Edinburgh passing through the area were made possible by the introduction of High-Speed Trains (HSTs) from 12th September 1977. In 1981 the East Coast Main Line became part of the InterCity sector of British Rail.

In 1982 Dr. David Serpell, a Civil Servant, published his report relating to the future of British Rail to cut the costs of the nationalised industry. Fortunately, it was not adopted as it would have removed the entire East Coast Main Line north of Newcastle, leaving the area covered by this album totally devoid of railways. Within a few years of its publication the entire rail network was attracting major growth through the business sectors.

On 27th July 1984, the Secretary of State authorised the electrification of the East Coast Main Line north of Hitchin (some of the London suburban services from Kings Cross were already electrified as far as Hitchin). Work gradually progressed northwards, with power being switched on in the Borders in March 1991. The first electric train between Edinburgh and London (and vice versa) ran on 12 June 1991. Electrification is by the 25kV AC overhead line system.

Privatisation of British Rail took place between 1994 and 1997. Local services were operated by Regional Railways prior to privatisation and afterwards by Arriva Trains Northern (1997 – 2004), Northern Rail (Serco / Abellio 2004 – 2016) and Northern (2016+). The East Coast Main Line trains are currently operated by London North Eastern Railway (LNER) a Government-owned company which took over the franchise in June 2018 and should not be confused with the earlier LNER company that operated the route between 1923 and 1948. Previously these services were provided by GNER (1996-2007), National Express (2007-2009), East Coast Trains (2009-2015) and Virgin Trains East Coast (2015-2018). CrossCountry trains also operate over the route.

The Seahouses Branch

The North Sunderland Railway was an independent railway built by the local business interests to provide a link between the NER line at Chathill and Seahouses which had seen the building of a new north pier in 1885 enabling it to develop into an important fishing port. Although the line received the Royal Assent in 1892 it was not until the passing of the Light Railway Act in 1896 that new railways of lighter construction were permitted to be built. Work on the four-mile line commenced on 13th November 1896 and it opened for goods traffic on 1st August 1898. The line did not open for passenger traffic until 18th December 1898. Plans for a station at Fleetham and a branch to Bamburgh, famous for its castle, from the terminus at Seahouses never materialised although a siding to serve Pasture Hill Quarry was installed.

The line obtained a Manning Wardle steam locomotive *Bamburgh* on hire purchase and this was the branch line locomotive for many years. In 1931, it trialled a diesel locomotive from Armstrong Whitworth and in 1933 it purchased an 0-4-0DE from them which was *The Lady Armstrong* named after the wife of Lord Armstrong. Coaching stock was always second hand and no more than three coaches were in use at any one time.

The line had little money and in 1939 due to debts owed the LNER took it over. Passing to British Railways in 1948, the last trains ran on 27th October 1951.

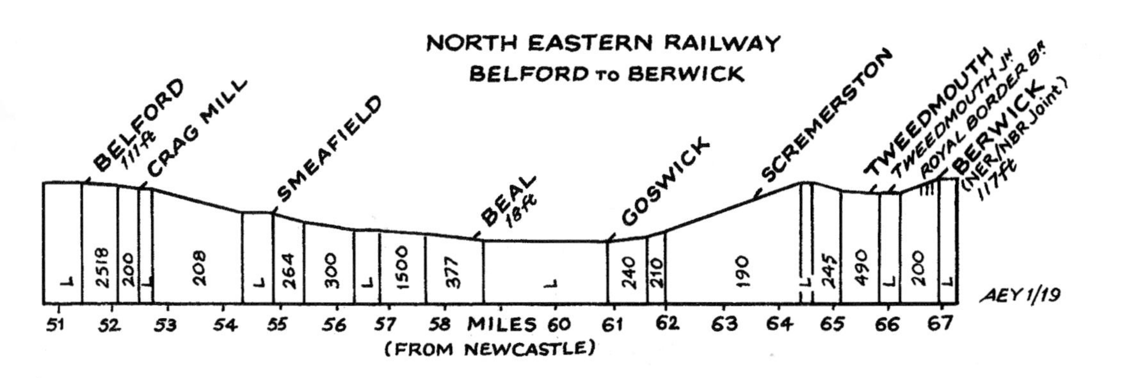

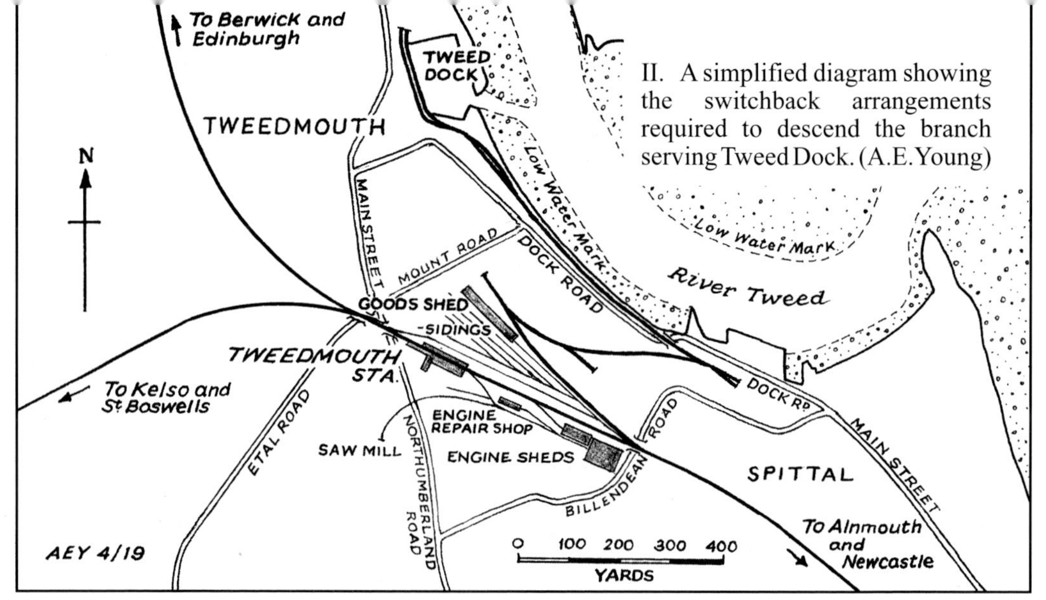

II. A simplified diagram showing the switchback arrangements required to descend the branch serving Tweed Dock. (A.E.Young)

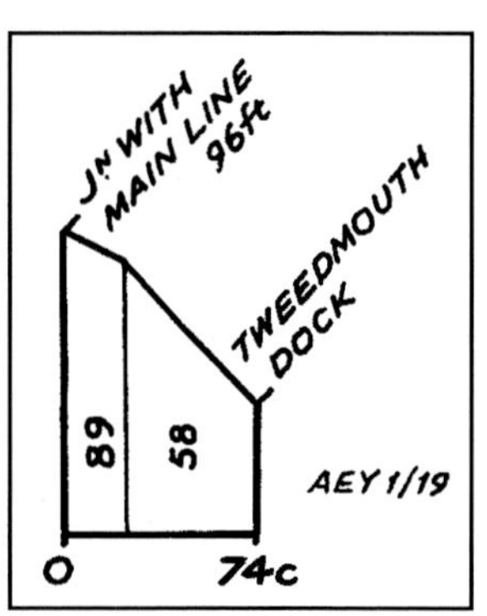

The Tweed Dock Branch

In the early 18th century Berwick was an important port, with ships carrying salmon from the river and other commodities away to market in London and elsewhere. By the middle of the 19th century the port had lost considerable traffic to others such as Leith and so new facilities were planned for the south bank at Tweedmouth in 1862. Construction began in 1873, the new facilities becoming Tweed Dock following its opening in 1876. A freight-only branch line was provided by the NER and was constructed in a zig-zag style more often associated with mountainous regions in South America and elsewhere. This required the construction of two major viaducts of which only one remains today. The line was officially opened on 16th October 1878. Trains had to reverse twice and the steep gradients restricted loads to no more than four wagons at a time. The branch was worked by the Tweedmouth Yard Pilot. It was not a great success and failed to serve other industrial companies on the south shore including gas, chemical, fertiliser works that could have provided additional traffic. The Tweed Dock branch closed to traffic in 1964 and was removed in 1965.

PASSENGER SERVICES

The Main Line

The Newcastle and Berwick Railway (N&BR) opened in 1847. It was built to link major conurbations and did not bother with local requirements. It failed to pass through Alnwick so Alnmouth became the more important station. Between Newcastle and Alnmouth there is still the skeleton of a local service but between Alnmouth and Berwick, there are only two substantial villages, Embleton and Belford. Embleton it ignored and at Belford the station was a mile from the village with the local lord's estate and, more recently, a bypass between them. The minimal local service from Newcastle ends at Chathill and is run by Northern. ScotRail has been talking for some years about improving local services between Edinburgh and Berwick and the logic would be to take them through to Newcastle but they cannot because it is outside their franchise area. Express trains stop at Berwick and Alnmouth only and not always at both stations. Main line services are provided by LNER, CrossCountry and TransPennine franchises.

The ECML has hosted some of Britain's fastest trains spurred on by competition with the West Coast Main Line. 'Flying Scotsman', 'Talisman', 'Elizabethan', 'Queen of Scots' are all famous names hauled by prime locomotives: NER Atlantics, LNER Pacifics, BR Deltics, InterCity 125, 91 class Intercity 225 and Hitachi 'Azumas'. Weekday intercity trains from Newcastle to Edinburgh have increased from 17 in 1961 to over 40 in 2019. However, this is being written

YORK, NEWCASTLE, & BERWICK RAILWAY.

STATIONS.	UP TRAINS FROM BERWICK TO YORK. 1	2	3	4	5	6	7	8	9		10	SUNDAYS. 11	12	13	14	15	16	17	18	FARES. 1st clas	2nd clas	3rd clas	4th Class
				Expr:		Mail					Mail				Mail				Mail				Id.m.
LEAVE			A.M.	a.m.	a.m.	a. m.			p.m.		p.m.			a.m.	a.m.			p.m.	p.m.	s. d.	s. d.	s. d.	s. d.
Glasgow	....	....	....	8 0	....	....	....	....	....	....	4 0	....	....	....	....	....	....	....	....	....	....	....	....
Edinburgh	....	....	....	9 45	8 0	11 0	....	....	....	....	6 0	....	....	....	11 0	....	....	....	6 0	....	....	....	....
			1 2 3 Cl	1 Class	1 2 3 Class	1 2 Class			1 2 3 Cl		1 2 Class			1 2 3 Class	1 2 Class			1 2 3 Cl	1 2 Class				
			a.m.	a.m.	a.m.	a.m.			p.m.		p.m.			a.m.	p.m.			p.m.	p.m.				
Berwick	....	....	7 15	11 20	10 45	1 15	....	....	5 30	....	8 35	....	....	7 0	1 15	....	....	5 15	8 35	....	....	....	....
Tweedmouth	....	....	7 17	....	10 47	1 17	....	....	5 32	....	8 37	....	....	7 2	1 17	....	....	5 17	8 37	0 6	0 3	....	0 2
Scremerston	....	....	7 22	....	10 52	....	....	....	5 37	....	....	....	....	7 7	....	....	....	5 22	....	1 0	0 8	....	0 6
Beal	....	....	7 32	....	11 2	....	....	....	5 47	....	....	....	....	7 17	....	....	....	5 32	....	1 9	1 3	....	0 9½
Belford	....	....	7 48	....	11 18	1 43	....	....	6 3	....	9 2	....	....	7 34	1 43	....	....	5 49	9 2	3 6	2 0	....	1 4½
Lucker	....	....	7 55	....	11 25	....	....	....	6 8	....	....	....	....	7 41	....	....	....	5 56	....	4 0	2 6	....	1 6¾
Chat Hill	....	....	8 2	....	11 32	....	....	....	6 15	....	....	....	....	7 48	....	....	....	6 3	....	4 6	2 9	....	1 9¼
Christon Bank	....	....	8 7	....	11 37	....	....	....	6 21	....	....	....	....	7 54	....	....	....	6 10	....	5 0	3 3	....	2 0¾
Longhoughton	....	....	8 24	....	11 54	....	....	....	6 35	....	....	....	....	8 11	....	....	....	6 27	....	6 6	3 9	....	2 6½
Lesbury. Alnwick	....	....	8 29	11 55	11 59	2 15	....	....	6 42	....	9 32	....	....	8 17	2 15	....	....	6 33	9 32	7 0	4 3	....	2 8½
Warkworth	....	....	8 42	....	12 12	....	....	....	6 54	....	....	....	....	8 30	....	....	....	6 46	....	7 6	4 9	....	3 0¾
Acklington	....	....	8 52	....	12 21	2 30	....	....	7 4	....	9 47	....	....	8 40	2 30	....	....	6 56	9 47	8 6	5 0	....	3 3½
Widdrington	....	....	9 3	....	12 33	....	....	....	7 14	....	....	....	....	8 52	....	....	....	7 8	....	9 6	5 9	....	3 8¼
Longhirst	....	....	9 11	....	12 41	....	....	....	7 23	....	....	....	....	9 0	....	....	....	7 16	....	10 0	6 3	....	3 11½
Morpeth	....	....	9 19	12 25	12 49	2 55	....	....	7 33	....	10 10	....	....	9 9	2 55	....	....	7 25	10 10	11 0	6 9	....	4 3
Netherton	....	....	9 28	....	12 58	....	....	....	7 43	....	....	....	....	9 18	....	....	....	7 34	....	11 6	6 9	....	4 5¼
Cramlington	....	....	9 40	....	1 10	....	....	....	7 53	....	....	....	....	9 30	....	....	....	7 46	....	12 0	7 3	....	4 9¾
Killingworth	....	....	9 50	....	1 20	....	....	....	8 2	....	....	....	....	9 41	....	....	....	7 57	....	13 0	7 9	....	5 2
ARRIVE AT										....	....	....	....										
Newcastle	....	....	10 15	1 5	1 45	3 30	....	....	8 15	....	....	....	....	10 0	3 30	....	....	8 15	10 45	14 0	8 9	....	5 7½

YORK, NEWCASTLE, & BERWICK RAILWAY.

STATIONS.	DOWN TRAINS FROM YORK TO BERWICK. 1	2	3	4	5	6	7	8	9		10	SUNDAYS. 11	12	13	14	15	16	17	18	FARES. 1st clas	2nd clas	3rd clas	4th clas
	1 2 3			1 2 3	1 2		1 2 3					1 2 3				1 2 3							
	A.M.	A.M.		A.M.	P.M.	P.M.	P.M.				P.M.	A.M.		A.M.		P.M			P. M.				
Newcastle	7 0	9 30	....	1 30	3 45	6 20	6 45	....	....	....	11 50	7 15	....	9 30	....	6 5	....	....	11 30	....	....	....	....
Killingworth	7 12	....	....	1 43	3 51	....	6 58	....	....	....	....	7 27	....	....	....	6 18	....	....	....	1 3	0 9	....	0 5½
Cramlington	7 21	....	....	1 52	4 2	....	7 7	....	....	....	....	7 37	....	....	....	6 27	....	....	....	1 9	1 3	....	0 9¾
Netherton	7 30	....	....	2 2	4 12	....	7 17	....	....	....	....	7 47	....	....	....	6 37	....	....	....	2 6	1 9	....	1 1¾
Morpeth	7 38	10 5	....	2 11	4 21	6 45	7 26	....	....	....	....	7 55	....	10 5	....	6 46	....	....	....	3 0	2 0	....	1 4½
Longhirst	7 45	....	....	2 18	4 34	....	7 33	....	....	....	....	8 4	....	....	....	6 54	....	....	....	4 0	2 6	....	1 8
Widdrington	7 58	....	....	2 32	4 42	....	7 47	....	....	....	....	8 12	....	....	....	7 7	....	....	....	5 0	3 0	....	1 11
Acklington	8 10	10 30	....	2 44	4 54	....	7 59	....	....	....	....	8 25	....	10 30	....	7 21	....	....	....	6 0	3 9	....	2 4½
Warkworth	8 18	....	....	2 53	5 5	....	8 8	....	....	....	....	8 31	....	....	....	7 28	....	....	....	6 6	4 0	....	2 6¾
Lesbury, Alnwick	8 29	10 45	....	3 4	5 14	7 10	8 19	....	....	....	....	8 41	....	10 45	....	7 39	....	....	....	7 6	4 6	....	2 10½
Longhoughton	8 35	....	....	3 11	5 21	....	8 26	....	....	....	....	8 47	....	....	....	7 46	....	....	....	8 0	5 0	....	3 1¼
Christon Bank	8 49	....	....	3 26	5 36	....	8 41	....	....	....	....	9 4	....	....	....	8 1	....	....	....	9 0	5 6	....	3 6¾
Chat-hill	8 57	....	....	3 34	5 44	....	3 49	....	....	....	....	9 8	....	....	....	8 9	....	....	....	9 6	6 0	....	3 9¼
Lucker	9 5	....	....	3 43	5 53	....	8 58	....	....	....	....	9 16	....	....	....	8 18	....	....	....	10 0	6 3	....	4 1
Belford	9 10	11 15	....	3 48	5 59	....	9 3	....	....	....	....	9 22	....	11 15	....	8 23	....	....	....	10 9	6 6	....	4 3½
Beal	9 26	....	....	4 5	6 18	....	9 20	....	....	....	....	9 40	....	....	....	8 40	....	....	....	12 0	7 6	....	4 10½
Scremerston	9 35	....	....	4 15	6 30	....	9 30	....	....	....	....	9 50	....	....	....	8 50	....	....	....	13 0	8 0	....	5 3½
Tweedmouth	9 43	11 43	....	4 23	6 38	....	9 38	....	....	....	....	9 58	....	11 43	....	8 58	....	....	....	13 6	8 6	....	5 5½
ARRIVE AT											A.M.								A.M.				
Berwick	0 45	11 45	....	4 25	6 40	8 5	9 40	....	....	....	2 0	10 0	....	11 45	....	9 0	....	....	2 0	14 0	8 9	....	5 7½
	P.M.	P.M.												P.M.									
Edinburgh	12 5	2 5	....	7 0	9 40	9 40	....	....	....	....	5 15	....	....	2 5	....	....	....	....	5 15	....	....	....	....
Glasgow	3 30	4 15	....	....	11 20	11 20	....	....	....	....	....	....	....	....	....	....	....	....	....	....	....	....	....

DURHAM.—Passengers can book at Durham for London (and places South of York at which the Up Express stops) by a Special Train leaving at 1 25 p.m.—The Down Express will stop at Belmont with Passengers from London and places South of York.

1849 timetable issued when the line was owned by the York, Newcastle & Berwick Railway.

during the Coronavirus pandemic and we will have to see what style of services settle down to be the new normal.

Chathill was the junction for the North Sunderland Railway (NSR) to Seahouses which closed in 1951. In the 1966 Transport Users' Consultative Committee report it was proposed to keep Chathill open and close Belford because Chathill had sold more tickets in the period of review, so today local trains stop at Chathill and then proceed empty to the closed station at Belford to cross over from the Down to the Up line and return. There was another unusual operating practice in NER days: local trains from Berwick and from Beal came down to Alnmouth and then reversed into Alnwick. Alnwick was the major shopping centre and when this practice was stopped, by 1920, a shopper from, say, Longhoughton, about four miles from Alnwick had to take a train to Alnmouth and change and the process then was reversed on the return journey. Longhoughton closed during World War II though there were probably some unofficial calls for service personnel at Boulmer airfield. The station closed finally on 18th June 1962 but appeared in the summer 1962 timetable with 'phantom' trains. The last train to stop at this station was probably an excursion on 3rd June 1963.

North Sunderland Railway

Initially, the service was seven trains a day with no Sunday service. After World War I it dropped to six services starting and finishing at Seahouses. North Sunderland station first appeared in the timetables in the 1930s. In 1934 a Sunday service was started but this was not restored after being discontinued in World War II. The timetables indicated 15 minutes for four miles: an average of 16mph. In some years, the midday train on Saturdays and then Mondays and Thursdays were about 30 minutes later. The first train from Seahouses was a 'Parliamentary, with 3rd class; other trains had 2nd and 3rd class. After complaints, two compartments of 2nd class coach no. 2 were designated 1st class. One suspects the ride was the same whatever the class. Fish traffic was attached to passenger trains as appropriate. The second train of the day in each direction was a mixed train. Sometimes the unfitted trucks were placed between the locomotive and the carriages! On arrival at Chathill the train went into the bay platform. When passengers had disembarked the locomotive pushed its train out, ran around it and pushed it back into the bay to await the next departure. There were repeated complaints about fly shunting for which there was no authorisation. The coaches were all second-hand four and six wheel designs and, over the years, came from the Highland Railway, the GER and the NER. The timetables gave early and late connections for both Newcastle and Berwick to Seahouses. The NSR always waited for delayed main line trains. Through tickets and season tickets were issued for local stations in the Newcastle and Berwick areas.

1932 publicity leaflet

NORTH SUNDERLAND RAILWAY.

TIME TABLE

From 14th SEPTEMBER, 1931, to 30th APRIL, 1932.

		A.M.	A.M.	P.M.	P.M.	P.M.
SEAHOUSES	dep.	*7 38	9 20	1 10	4 10	6 30
CHATHILL	arr.	7 48	9 35	1 25	4 25	6 45

		A.M.	A.M.	P.M.	P.M.	P.M.
CHATHILL	dep.	*8 12	10 48	†2 0	†5 42	†6 55
SEAHOUSES	arr.	8 27	11 3	2 15	5 57	7 10

* Third Class (Parliamentary) Train.

† The 9.30 a.m., 12.22, 4.0 and 5.38 p.m. Express Trains from Newcastle stop at Chathill, connections arrive at Seahouses at 11.3 a.m., 2.15, 5.57 and 7.10 p.m.

THROUGH SERVICE.

In connection with L.N.E.R.

		A.M.	A.M.	P.M.	P.M.	E P.M.
Seahouses	dep	7 38	9 20	1 10	4 10	6 30
Chathill	arr.	7 48	9 35	1 25	4 25	6 45
Alnmouth	"	8 32	10 3	2 19	5 22	9 57
Alnwick	"	8 54	10 27	2 43	5 37	10 15
Morpeth	"	9 15	10 29	3 20	6 7	10 27
Newcastle	"	9 45	10 56	3 50	6 39	11 2
Belford	"	8 18	10 41	1 46	5 28	7 2
Berwick	"	9 0	11 7	2 6	5 50	7 22
Edinburgh	"		P.M. 12 42	3 25	8 26	8 42

		A.M.	A.M.	A.M.	P.M.	P.M.
Edinburgh	dep.		7 40	10 25	2 35	
Berwick	"	7 23	9 10	P.M. 1 13	4 54	
Belford	"	7 56	9 33	1 46	5 27	
Newcastle	"	6 12	9 20	12 22	4 0	5 38
Morpeth	"	6 56	9 49	12 52	4 28	6 9
Alnwick	"	7 20	9 55	1 5	4 48	6 22
Alnmouth	"	7 38	10 19	1 28	5 9	6 35
Chathill	"	8 12	10 48	2 0	5 42	6 55
Seahouses	arr.	8 27	11 3	2 15	5 57	7 10

E—L.N.E.R train from Berwick calls at Chathill at 9.42 p.m. when required.

Fares.

	SINGLE.						RETURN.					
	1st Class		2nd Class		3rd Class Parliamentary		1st Class		2nd Class		3rd Class Parliamentary	
	s.	d.	s.	d.	s.	d.	s.	d.	s.	d.	s.	d.
Seahouses to Chathill	1	2	0	11	0	9	2	4	1	10	1	6

Through Tickets

From Seahouses to:—	Experimental Fares				SINGLE.				RETURN.			
	3rd Class SINGLE		3rd Class RETURN		1st Class		2nd Class to Chathill, 3rd beyond		1st Class		2nd Class to Chathill 3rd beyond	
	s.	d.	s.	d.	s.	d.	s.	d.	s.	d.	s.	d.
Alnmouth	2	2	3	10	3	7	2	5	7	2	4	10
Alnwick	2	3	3	10	4	3	2	9	8	6	5	6
Belford					2	5	1	8	4	10	3	4
Berwick			*3	7	5	7	3	7	11	2	7	2
Heaton					10	6	6	6	21	0	13	0
Newcastle			*6	9	10	11	6	9	21	10	13	6
Tweedmouth					5	4	3	5	10	8	6	10
Monkseaton (via Hartley)					10	1	6	8	20	2	12	6
Monkseaton (via Heaton)					12	2	7	6	24	4	15	0
Wallsend (via Heaton)					10	11	6	9	21	10	13	6
Tyne Dock and South Shields					13	1	8	1	26	2	16	2

* Cheap tickets Thursdays and Saturdays, single fare for double journey.

PERIODICAL OR SEASON TICKETS.

SEAHOUSES TO CHATHILL.

12 MONTHS.		6 MONTHS.		3 MONTHS.		2 MONTHS.		1 MONTH.		14 DAYS.	
1st Class	3rd Class	1st Class	3rd Class	1st Class	3rd Class	1st Class	3rd Class	1st Class	3rd Class	1st Class	3rd Class
£ s. d.	£ s. d.	£ s. d.	£ s. d.	£ s. d.	£ s. d.	£ s. d.	£ s. d.	£ s. d.	£ s. d.	£ s. d.	£ s. d.
11 12 6	7 14 6	6 7 6	4 5 6	3 9 9	2 6 6	2 10 3	1 13 9	1 11 6	1 1 0	1 0 3	0 13 6

Periodical Tickets are issued at half-price to children under 15 years of age, and also to scholars, students, and apprentices learning a profession or trade, and not in receipt of salary, up to 18 years of age, on production by them of a Certificate from the Master of the School, the Principal of the College, or their Employer, as the case may be. A deposit of 5s. is required in respect of Periodical Tickets taken for a period of less than 3 months, such deposit will be returned to the Ticket Holder provided the ticket be given up on expiry.

The issuing of Tickets to Passengers to places off this Company's line is an arrangement made for the greater convenience of the public; but the Company will not be held responsible for the non-arrival of this Company's own trains in time for any nominally corresponding train on the London & North Eastern Company's line, nor for any delay, detention, or other loss or injury whatsoever which may arise therefrom, or for the acts or defaults of other parties, nor for the correctness of the times over the London & North Eastern Company's line.

PARCELS sent by Passenger Trains are received by the Company to be carried only on the same conditions relative to the times of the trains as stated in the notice above given.

N.B.—The hours or times stated in these Tables are appointed as those at which it is intended, as far as circumstances will permit, the Passenger Trains should depart from and arrive at Seahouses and Chathill respectively, but their departure or arrival at the times stated is not guaranteed, nor will the Company, under any circumstances, be held responsible for delay or detention, however occasioned, or any consequences arising therefrom.

61, Westgate Road, Newcastle-on-Tyne,
14th September, 1931.

RICHARD SMITH, Secretary.

JOHN BELL & CO., Printers, Railway Lane, Pilgrim Street, Newcastle.

ALNMOUTH FOR ALNWICK

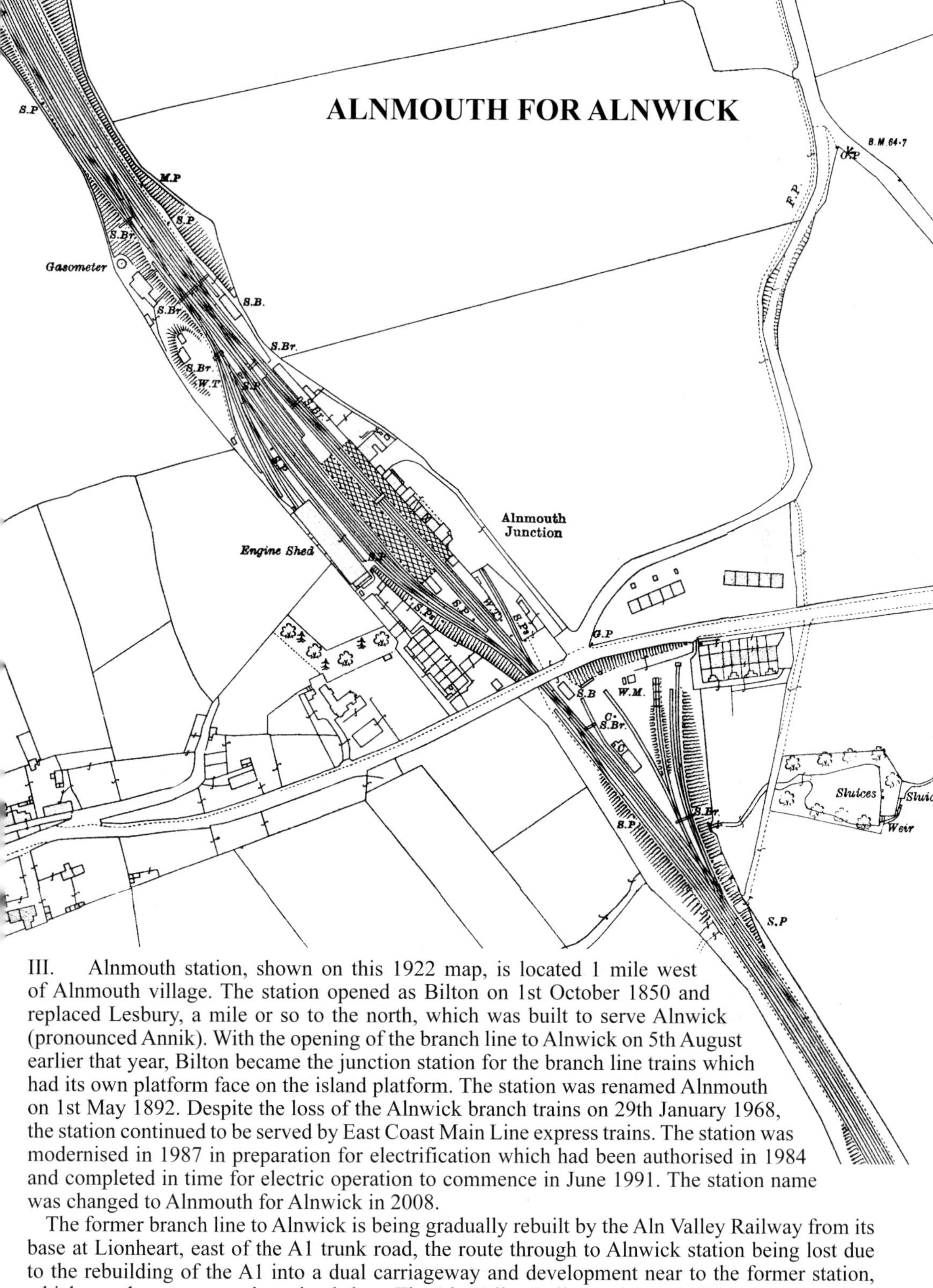

III. Alnmouth station, shown on this 1922 map, is located 1 mile west of Alnmouth village. The station opened as Bilton on 1st October 1850 and replaced Lesbury, a mile or so to the north, which was built to serve Alnwick (pronounced Annik). With the opening of the branch line to Alnwick on 5th August earlier that year, Bilton became the junction station for the branch line trains which had its own platform face on the island platform. The station was renamed Alnmouth on 1st May 1892. Despite the loss of the Alnwick branch trains on 29th January 1968, the station continued to be served by East Coast Main Line express trains. The station was modernised in 1987 in preparation for electrification which had been authorised in 1984 and completed in time for electric operation to commence in June 1991. The station name was changed to Alnmouth for Alnwick in 2008.

The former branch line to Alnwick is being gradually rebuilt by the Aln Valley Railway from its base at Lionheart, east of the A1 trunk road, the route through to Alnwick station being lost due to the rebuilding of the A1 into a dual carriageway and development near to the former station, which now houses a very large bookshop. The Aln Valley Railway aims to build its own station at Alnmouth adjacent to the Network Rail facility on land formerly occupied by the engine shed and sidings. Work began on site at Lionheart only in 2010 and in that time much has been accomplished by the society in its efforts to extend the operating line closer to Alnmouth.

1. We are looking south to the station through a forest of signals. The NER did not like ground signals. From left to right in this 1907 view is: the signal box, the main building with express lines in the centre and the branch trains to Alnwick on the right side of the Down platform. George Hudson was in trouble with the N&BR Board over his expenditures so Alnmouth never got a magnificent structure like many of the other wayside stops. Finally on the right is the engine shed with a row of railway cottages above and behind it. (J.F.Mallon coll./NERA)

2. NER class R (later D20) 4-4-0 no. 723 was on an Up stopping train to Newcastle. In their day, these were the crack express locomotives of the NER. In their last days they ended up handling Newcastle to Alnwick via Alnmouth trains. No. 723 was built at Gateshead in November 1906 but was withdrawn in May 1949 before receiving its BR number 62377. (A.E.Young coll.)

3. The road bridge to the south of the station was a convenient place to watch and photograph until the overhead catenary went up in 1991. This was 1967 and the end of regular steam working was nigh. The station, however, remained in the Victorian era and was a little shabby too with its ugly footbridge. (J.C.Dean/NERA)

More photographs of Alnmouth can be seen in our *Newcastle to Alnmouth* album.

4. The goods yard was south of the road bridge and had several short sidings and an elevated coal drop. There was a weighbridge and a large crane here photographed in 1967. North of the station were longer sidings that could take a whole train. (J.C.Dean/NERA)

5. The photographer was in the North signal box as class A4 4-6-2 no. 4469 (later no. 60006) *Sir Ralph Wedgwood* came through with the Up 'Flying Scotsman' on 11th August 1939. Beyond the end of the last carriage was the row of railway cottages in the V junction between the main line and the Alnwick branch. (R.J.Buckley/Initial Photographics)

6. This was the interior of the North signal box in December 1968 when Alnmouth took over control of the signals between Alnmouth and Little Mill. (J.M.Boyes/ARPT)

7. The station was completely rebuilt in 1989 before the main line was electrified. The branch to Alnwick was closed on 28th January 1968 and the lines through the station are now only plain track. An InterCity 125 is passing on an Up train. (G.W.Morrison)

8. The station was reconstructed with the buildings much reduced but with lifts and a new footbridge. On 15th September 2013, class 91 Bo-BoWE no. 91114 *Durham Cathedral* is propelling its London-bound train out of the station. (D.A.Lovett)

Alnmouth Engine Shed

9. Situated on the west side of the station, the engine shed appears empty. To the right was an inclined coaling siding. When coal wagons were shunted on to the siding, extra empty wagons were added so that the locomotive did not run on to the incline. Coaling was by hand so the side doors of the coal wagons and the tender of the locomotive being coaled had to line up. 'Loco coal' wagons were usually old stock and often wooden. The coal could have come from nearby Shilbottle colliery. Map III (preceding picture no. 1) shows the engine shed site adjacent to the station with the turntable located away from the shed. This is also indicated in map IV (overleaf) alongside the junction for the line to Alnwick. The two-road shed opened in 1876 and was a sub-shed of 52D Tweedmouth for most of its existence but was a sub-shed of 52B Heaton when it closed on 19th June 1966. (J.C.Dean/NERA)

3762 ALNWICK 3762
Alnwick TO Alnwick
BILTON JUN.
Bilton Jun. Bilton Jun.
Second Class N.E.R.
Issued subject to regulations in time tables

N.E.R. ALNWICK N.E.R
8922 Alnwick TO Alnwick 8922
ALNMOUTH
Alnmouth R Alnmouth
Fare 3d. Fare 3d.
THIRD CLASS THIRD
Issued subject to regulations in time tables

10. NER class M1 (LNER class D17/1) 4-4-0 no. 1621 has just 'coaled up' and is moving to a class K pick-up goods train. No. 1621 took part in the 1895 'Race to Aberdeen' and is now in the national collection at the Railway Museum, York. (R.J.Buckley/Initial Photographics)

11. The later NER class R (LNER class D20) 4-4-0 no. 62380 was on shed in the 1950s. Built in 1907 it was withdrawn in September 1954. Also in the photograph is BR2 type tender of a BR 4MT 2-6-0. No. 76024 was allocated to Alnmouth between 3rd May 1953 and 4th April 1954. (N.E.Stead coll./Transport Library)

12. On 18th September 1955, Ivatt 4MT 2-6-0 no. 43016 from Heaton (52B) and class J39 0-6-0 no. 64941 were on shed. Servicing was done on shed. Ash from the loco fires was dropped between the rails and then hand-carted away: like coaling, another mucky job! The turntable was at the Alnwick branch junction, outside the shed bounds and necessitated inefficient light engine movements.
(G.W.Morrison)

← July 1919

YORK, NEWCASTLE, MORPETH, ALNMOUTH, BERWICK, and EDINBURGH.—North Eastern.

Down.	Week Days.																		Sundays.						
	ngt	mrn	mn	mn	mrn	mrn	mrn	mrn	mrn	aft	aft	aft	aft	aft	aft	aft	aft	aft	mrn	mn	mn	mrn	mrn	aft	aft
534 York .... dep.	1124	1256	249	350	...	...	7 5	9 38	10 5	Arrives Amble at 1 51 aft., see page 559.	...	...	1250	216	...	245	5 35	6 25	1256	249	350	4 5	6 30	...	...
534 Darlington (B.T.) B	1035	1 56	...	456	...	7 49	9 3	...	1110		...	...	1 54	2 5	...	4 6	6 33	7 29	1 56	...	457	...	8 20	...	...
Newcastle (Cen.) .. dep.	1 15	2 58	444	630	8 0	9 35	1030	1123	1225		1255	1s30	3 0	4 8	5 7	553	7 33	8 45	2 58	444	620	8 0	1040	233	637
Manors East	mrn	...	...	...	8 2	...	1032	...	...		1257	1s32	3 2		...	556		8 47	...	...	...	8 2	...	235	639
Heaton	...	...	...	636	8 7	...	1037	...	...		1 2	1s37	3 7		...	6 1		8 54	...	...	...	8 7	1045	240	644
Forest Hall	...	...	...	643	8 15	...	1044	...	...		1 3	1s44	3 14		...	6 9		9 1	...	...	...	8 14	...	247	651
Killingworth	...	...	...	647	8 19	...	1048	...	...		1 13	1s48	3 18		...	615		9 5	...	...	...	8 18	...	251	655
Annitsford	...	...	...	652	8 24	...	1053	...	...		1 18	1s53	3 23		...	621		9 10	...	...	635	8 23	...	256	7 0
Cramlington	...	...	...	657	8 30	...	1059	...	...		1 25	2s0	3 30		...	627		9 15	...	...	640	8 29	...	3 2	7 6
Plessey	...	...	...	...	8 35	...	11 3	...	...		1 30	2s5	3 35		...	632		s	...	...	...	8 34	...	3 6	710
Stannington	...	...	...	7 5	8 41	...	11 9	...	...		1 36	2s11	3 41		...	637		9 23	...	...	645	8 40	...	311	715
Morpeth 544, 638	...	...	...	717	8 55	9 59	1121	...	1252	1s15	1 48	2s18	3 54		533	650		9F35	...	...	658	8 49	11 9	318	724
Pegswood, for Bothal	...	...	...	...	9 0	...	1125	...	...	1s19	1 52		3 58		...	654		9 39	...	...	...	8 53	...	...	728
Longhirst	...	...	...	...	9 4	...	1129	...	...	1s23	1 57	Stop	4 3		...	659		9 44	...	...	...	8 57	...	...	732
Widdrington	...	...	...	...	9 11	...	1136	...	...	1s30	2 4	...	4 10		...	7 7		9 52	...	...	...	9 5	...	...	740
Chevington 560	...	...	...	...	9 18	...	1143	...	...	1s36	2 12	...	4 18		548	715		9 59	...	...	...	9 11	...	...	747
Acklington, for Felton	...	...	...	733	9 24	...	12T3	...	...		2 19	...	4 51	Dining Car Express.	554	...	Dining Car Express.	10 5	...	...	715	9 18	1124	...	754
Warkworth	...	...	...	739	9 31	...	12 8	...	...	Stop	2 26	...	4 57		6 0	...		1013	...	...	...	9 26	1131	...	8 1
Alnmouth 553 .... arr.	...	...	...	745	9 36	1021	1214	...	1 16	...	2 33	...	5 3		6 6	...		1020	...	...	726	9 32	1137	...	8 7
553 Alnwick .... arr.	...	...	...	757	9 52	1042	1224	...	1 32	aft	2 45	aft	5 14		617	...		1032	...	...	747	9 47	1151	...	820
Alnmouth .... dep.	...	...	...	754	9 41	1024	Stop	...	1 20	1 30	...	2 55	...		630	...		...	...	...	728	9 34	1139	...	8 9
Longhoughton	...	...	...	...	9 48	...		...	...	1 36	...	3 1	...		636	...		...	...	...	...	9 41	...	...	815
Little Mill	...	...	...	...	9 55	...		...	...	1 41	...	3 6	...		641	...		...	...	...	...	9 47	...	...	821
Christon Bank *	...	...	...	...	10 2	...		...	...	1 48	...	3 13	...		648	...		...	...	...	...	9 54	...	...	828
Chathill 540	...	...	...	810	10 9	...		...	1 39	1 53	...	3 19	...		653	...		...	...	...	745	10 1	1155	...	834
Newham	...	...	...	...	1014	...		...	...	1 58	...	3 24	...		658	...		...	...	...	...	10 6	...	...	838
Lucker †	...	...	...	...	1019	...		...	...	2 3	...	3 29	...		7 3	...		...	...	...	...	1011	...	...	843
Belford	...	...	...	820	1026	1048	...	...	1 50	2 8	...	3 37	...		7 8	...		...	...	...	756	1018	12 5	...	850
Smeafield	...	...	...	...	d	...	mrn	...	...	...	...	...	...		d	...		...	...	...	...	...	...	...	...
Beal ‡	...	...	...	831	1038	11 1	11 7	...	...	2 19	...	3 48	...		719	...		...	...	...	8 7	1031	1219	...	9 2
Goswick	...	...	...	836	...	...	1112	...	...	2 23	...	3 52	...		723	...		...	...	...	...	1037	...	...	9 7
Scremerston	...	...	...	...	...	...	1118	...	...	2 29	...	3 58	...		729	...		...	...	...	...	1043	...	...	913
Tweedmouth 542	...	...	...	855	...	...	1124	...	2 13	2 38	...	4 6	...		735	...		...	...	...	829	1055	...	...	922
Berwick 542, 624 arr.	...	4 22	...	858	...	1114	...	...	2 16	2 41	...	4 10	...	533	...	...	8 54	...	4 22	...	832	11 0	1232	...	927
624 Edinburgh (W.) arr.	4 0	5 45	730	...	...	1251	...	1 55	3 53	...	...	...	...	7 0	...	...	1020	...	5 45	730	...	...	...	...	...

Up.	Week Days.																	Sundays.					
	mrn	mrn	mrn	mrn	mrn	mrn	aft	mrn	aft	aft	aft	aft	aft	aft	aft	aft	aft	mrn	aft	aft	aft	aft	aft
625 Edinburgh (W.) dep.	...	...	...	...	...	10 0		1020	...	...	1230	...	2 25	...	6 45	10 0	...	...	...	...	...	6 45	10 0
Berwick .... dep.	...	...	...	7 20	9 10	1120		12 5	...	1 10	1 56	2 20	4 21	4 50	8 29	...	1138	6 5	4 20	5 50	...	8 29	...
Tweedmouth	...	...	...	7 24	9 14		Starts from Amble at 12 23 aft., see page 559.	...	...	1 14		2 24	4 27	4 54	...	...		6 9	...	5 54	...	...	...
Scremerston	...	...	...	7 29	9 19			...	...	1 19		2 30	...	4 59	...	...		6 15	...	6 0	...	...	...
Goswick	...	...	...	7 34	9 24			...	...	1 24		2 36	...	5 4	...	...		6 20	...	6 6	...	...	...
Beal ‡	...	...	...	7 39	9 29			...	...	1 29		2 41	...	5 9	...	...		6 25	...	6 12	...	...	...
Smeafield	...	...	...	b	...			...	...	...		Sig.	...	d	...	...		...	...	...	...	...	...
Belford	...	...	...	7 54	9 43			1226	...	1 42		2 54	4 50	5 24	...	...	Leaves Aberdeen at 6 35 aft.	6 36	4 45	6 23	...	...	...
Lucker †	...	...	...	7 59	9 48			...	...	1 47		3 0	...	5 29	...	...		6 41	...	6 28	...	...	...
Newham	...	...	...	8 3	9 52			...	...	1 51		3 5	...	5 33	...	...		6 46	...	6 33	...	...	...
Chathill 540	...	...	...	8 7	9 57			1237	...	1 54		3 9	5 2	5 36	...	...		6 50	4 57	6 37	...	...	...
Christon Bank *	...	...	...	8 14	10 4			...	...	2 1		3 16	...	5 43	...	...		6 56	...	6 44	...	...	...
Little Mill	...	...	...	8 22	1012			...	...	2 9		3 24	...	5 52	...	...		7 4	...	6 52	...	...	...
Longhoughton	...	...	...	8 27	1017			...	...	2 14		3 29	...	5 58	...	...		7 9	...	6 58	...	...	...
Alnmouth 553 .... arr.	...	...	...	8 35	1023			1251	...	2 19		3 35	5 21	6 4	9 13	...		7 14	5 16	7 3	...	9 13	...
553 Alnwick ...... dep.	...	6 55	7 55	8 35	1010			1235		2 35			5 5	6 30	8 53	...	...	7 0	5 0	6 50	...	8 53	...
Alnmouth .... dep.	...	7 3	8 5	8 45	1036			1256		2 47			5 25	6 45	9 19	...	...	7 16	5 20	7 7	...	9 19	...
Warkworth	...	7 9	8 11	8 53	1043			...		2 54			5 33	6 53	...	...	...	7 23	5 28	7 15	...	...	...
Acklington, for Felton.	...	7 16	8 18	9 1	1050	Luncheon Car Express.		...	Saturdays only.	3 1	Luncheon Car Express.	Saturdays only.	5 41	7 1	...	...	...	7 32	5 36	7 24	...	...	...
Chevington 560	...	7 23	8 24	...	1057		1239	...		3 7			5 49	7 10	...	...	...	7 39	...	7 32	...	...	...
Widdrington	...	7 32	...	...	11 4		1246	...		3 14			...	7 17	...	...	...	7 46	...	7 39	...	...	...
Longhirst	...	7 38	...	9 13	1111		1252	...		3 21			...	7 24	...	...	...	7 53	...	7 46	...	...	...
Pegswood, for Bothal	...	7 42	...	...	1115		1256	...		3 25			...	7 28	...	...	...	7 57	...	7 50	...	...	...
Morpeth 544, 638	6 57	7 51	8 40	9 23	1124		1 0	1 22	3 8	3 34		...	6 10	7 37	9 53	...	...	8 7	6 6	7 59	8 15	9 53	...
Stannington	7 3	7 57	...	...	1130			...	3 14	3 40		...	...	7 43	...	...	...	8 14	...	...	8 21	...	...
Plessey	...	8 2	...	...	1135			...	3 19	3 45		...	...	7 48	...	...	...	8 19	...	...	8 26	...	...
Cramlington	7 10	8 6	8 53	...	1140		Saturdays only.	...	3 24	3 49		...	...	7 52	...	...	...	8 24	...	...	8 30	...	...
Annitsford	7 15	8 11	8 58	...	1146			...	3 30	3 54		...	...	7 58	...	...	...	8 29	...	...	8 35	...	...
Killingworth	7 20	8 16	9 3	...	1151			...	3 35	3 59		...	...	8 3	...	...	...	8 34	...	...	8 40	...	...
Forest Hall	7 24	8 20	...	...	1155			...	3 39	4 3		...	...	8 7	...	...	...	8 38	...	...	8 44	...	...
Heaton	7 31	8 26	...	...	12 2			...	3 46	4 10		...	...	8 15	...	...	...	8 45	...	8 20	8 51	...	...
Manors East	7 36	8 32	9 15	9 48	12 9			...	3 52	4 17		...	...	8 21	...	...	...	8 52	...	8 26	8 57	...	...
Newcastle (C.) 536 arr.	7 39	8 35	9 18	9 51	1212	1246		1 50	3 55	4 20	3 16	...	6 40	8 24	1025	1243	1 0	8 55	6 35	8 29	9 0	1025	1243
536 Darlington § .. arr.	8 44	...	1041	11 4	1 21	1 46	...	3 25	...	5 45	4 16	...	8 16	1139	1154	1 43	...	1110	8 5	...	1139	1154	1 43
536 York .... "	9 45	...	1148	12 9	2 29	2 44	...	4 53	...	6 47	5 14	...	8 40	1244	1259	2 40	2 56	1220	9 16	...	1244	1259	2 40

B Leaves Darlington at 11 34 aft. on Sundays. b Stops on Mondays, Tuesdays, and Saturdays. d Stops on Tuesdays and Saturdays when required. F Arrives Morpeth at 9 29 aft. s Saturdays only. s Stops on Saturdays only. T Arrives Acklington at 11 49 mrn. * Station for Embleton (1½ miles). † Station for Bamburgh (3 miles). ‡ Station for Holy Island (4 miles) and Lowick (4 miles). § Bank Top Station.

NORTH OF ALNMOUTH

Alnwick Junction

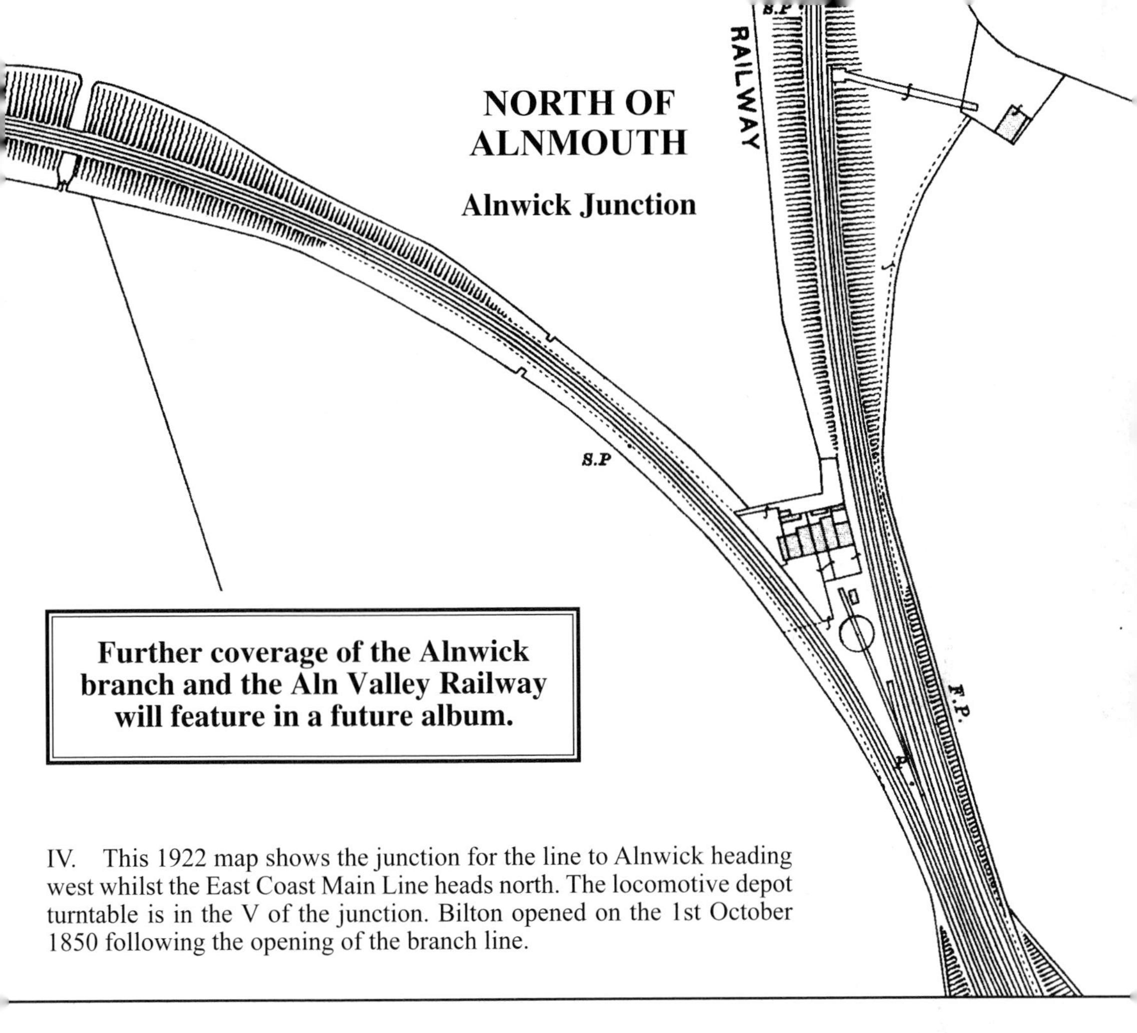

Further coverage of the Alnwick branch and the Aln Valley Railway will feature in a future album.

IV. This 1922 map shows the junction for the line to Alnwick heading west whilst the East Coast Main Line heads north. The locomotive depot turntable is in the V of the junction. Bilton opened on the 1st October 1850 following the opening of the branch line.

13. A row of railway cottages previously seen in picture 5 stood at the junction. In the foreground were the remains of the 42ft 2in diameter turntable pit. It was 1968 and a Metro-Cammell DMU (later class 101) was en-route to Alnwick. (ARPT)

Aln Valley Railway

14. This preservation society is re-laying the branch from Alnmouth to Alnwick. Working back from Alnwick Lionheart station in September 2019 it had reached Grayrigg Halt. On the 14th 0-6-0ST no. 60 (Hunslet 3686 of 1948) was the first steam engine to reach the halt. (P.Murphy/AVR)

ALNWICK LIONHEART

15. The society opened the Lionheart station on 26th April 2017. Here no. 9 *Richboro* 0-6-0T (Hudswell Clarke 1243 of 1917), which was ultimately bought by the society in 2020, arrives at the station on 10th September 2019. (Ms C.Harrison)

ALNWICK

16. There were two stations at Alnwick. The first (1850-87) is the cattle dock in this 1946 photograph. The main station building is now the famous Barter Bookshop. The pillar in the background has the Percy Lion on the top. It is said that this was erected by the Duke of Northumberland's tenants in gratitude that he had not raised their rents. He said that if they could afford to pay for the column they could pay higher rents and put them up! This was a terminus station; trains from Alnmouth were on the right and trains to Wooler and Coldstream on the left.
(J.W.Sparrowe/R.S.Carpenter coll.)

September 1951

BRITISH RAILWAYS

TRAIN SERVICE
ALNMOUTH and ALNWICK
SEPTEMBER 10th 1951 until further notice

Table 73

WEEKDAYS

		pm	am		am	am	am	am	am	pm	pm				pm
London (King's Cross)	dep	8Z20	1 0	....	....	....	3 50	....	10 5	....	12 18	....	....	....	3Z30
York	"	1a13	5 4	..	..	6 40	10 5	11 32	2p2	2 50	4 12	..	..	..	7 16
Newcastle	"	3 11	6 52	....	7 15	9 28	12p21	1Ap20	4 18	5a7	6 5	....	....	....	10A0
				am					pm					pm	
Edinburgh	dep	..	..	..	..	6 55	10 25	..	2 30	..	..	..	..	8 0	..
Berwick	"	....	....	7 22	....	8 55	12p11	....	4 20	....	....	....	....	9 25	....
								SO							
		am	am	am	am	am	pm	pm	pm	pm	pm	pm	pm	pm	pm
ALNMOUTH	dep	6 30	7 42	8 30	9 0	10 25	1 21	2 41	5 23	6 12	7 10	8 45	9 40	10 17	11 27
ALNWICK	arr	6 37	7 49	8 37	9 7	10 32	1 28	2 48	5 30	6 19	7 17	8 52	9 47	10 24	11 34

WEEKDAYS

							SO								
		am	am	am	am	am	am	pm	pm	pm	pm	pm	pm	pm	pm
ALNWICK	dep	7 12	7A29	8 15	8 44	9 38	10A20	12 52	4A25	5 0	6 50	8 25	9 14	10 0	11 0
ALNMOUTH	arr	7 18	7 36	8 21	8 50	9 44	10 26	12 58	4 31	5 6	6 56	8 31	9 20	10 6	11 6
			am	am		am	am	pm	pm	pm			pm	pm	
Newcastle	arr	....	8 53	9 29	....	10F45	11 53	2d40	5 57	6 11	....	....	10S51	11 10	....
York	"	..	....	11 35	..	1 31	2 18	4 44	—	9 16	..	..	—	1K5	..
London (King's Cross)	"	....	2V6	3 29	....	....	5 50	9B55	....	3a6	....	....	....	6 5	....
		am			am	am		pm		pm	pm				
Berwick	arr	8 10	..	..	10 7	11 7	..	2 8	..	6 25	8w3	..	..	..	..
Edinburgh	"	9 26	....	....	....	12 41	....	3 35	....	9f2	10 0	....	....	....	....

A—Through Train between Newcastle and Alnwick B—Passengers can arrive King's Cross 8.10 pm by Pullman Car train, supplementary charge E—Also applies on Sunday nights F—On Saturdays arrives Newcastle 10.50 am K—On Sundays arrives York 1.11 am S or SO—Saturdays only V—By the Tees—Tyne Pullman from Newcastle, Saturdays excepted, supplementary charge. Z—Except Saturdays passengers can leave King's Cross 4.45 pm by Pullman Car train to Newcastle. Supplementary charge a—am d—On Thursdays and Saturdays arrives Newcastle 2.3 pm f—On Saturdays arrives Edinburgh 9.4 pm p—pm w—On Saturdays arrives Berwick 8.6 pm

The Aln Viaduct

17. We return to the ECML as class 24 Bo-BoDE no. D5071 crosses the 18-arch viaduct with a southbound empty coal train. The date was 5th May 1972. The viaduct is 1068ft long and has spans of 30ft with a maximum height of 75ft. The river spans were on shale and the others on clay but, looking north, the first, fourth and last piers needed piled foundations. (K.Gregory/ARPT)

18. A GNER high speed train with a class 43 Bo-BoDE at each end travels under the wires with an up train to Kings Cross. It is fair to say this was BR's most successful locomotive design. (G.W.Morrison)

LESBURY

V. Lesbury was built to serve the town of Alnwick three miles away and opened on 1st July 1847. A horse bus was provided from the station to Alnwick. It was a short-lived station as it was replaced by Bilton on 1st October 1850, following the opening of the branch line to Alnwick. Goods facilities were removed on the same day. Bilton station was renamed Alnmouth in 1892. The former station building at Lesbury remains in residential use. This extract is dated 1897.

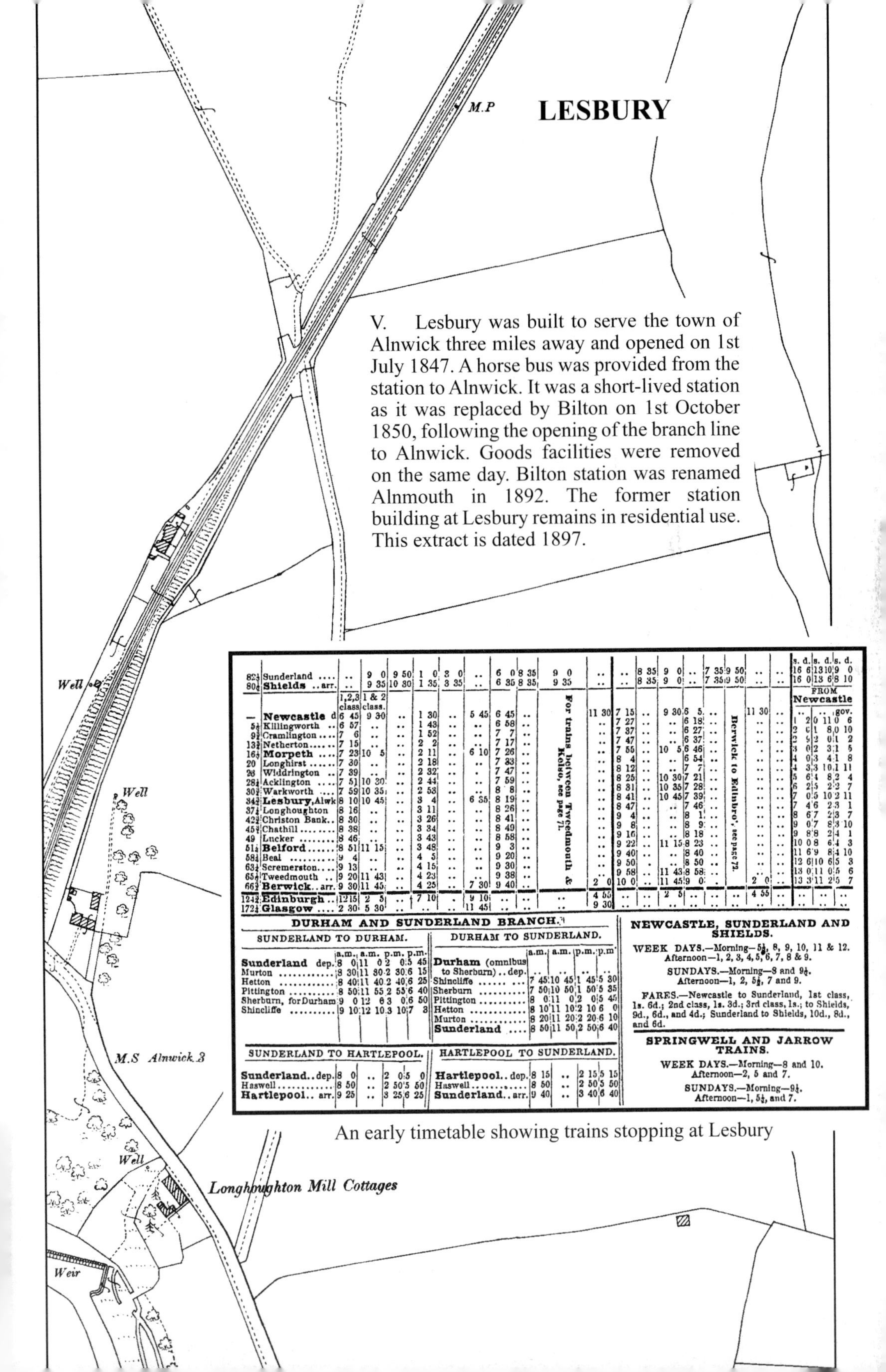

Miles	Station	1,2,3 class	1 & 2 class							For trains between Tweedmouth & Kelso, see page 71.	
82⅓	Sunderland	..	9 0	9 50	1 0	3 0	..	6 0	8 35	9 0	..
80⅙	**Shields** ..arr.	..	9 35	10 30	1 35	3 35	..	6 35	8 35	9 35	..
—	**Newcastle** d	6 45	9 30	..	1 30	..	5 45	6 45	..		11 30
5¼	Killingworth ..	6 57	..	..	1 43	..	..	6 58	..		..
9¾	Cramlington	7 6	..	..	1 52	..	..	7 7	..		..
13¾	Netherton......	7 15	..	..	2 2	..	..	7 17	..		..
16¼	**Morpeth**	7 23	10 5	..	2 11	..	6 10	7 26	..		..
20	Longhirst	7 30	..	..	2 18	..	..	7 33	..		..
23	Widdrington ..	7 39	..	..	2 32	..	.	7 47	..		..
28¼	Acklington	7 51	10 30	..	2 44	..	..	7 59	..		..
30¾	Warkworth	7 59	10 35	..	2 53	..	..	8 8	..		..
34¾	**Lesbury**, Alwk	8 10	10 45	..	3 4	..	6 35	8 19	..		..
37¼	Longhoughton	8 16	..	..	3 11	..	..	8 26	..		..
42¾	Christon Bank..	8 30	..	..	3 26	..	..	8 41	..		..
45¾	Chathill	8 38	..	..	3 34	..	..	8 49	..		..
49	Lucker	8 46	..	..	3 43	..	..	8 58	..		..
51¼	**Belford**......	8 51	11 15	..	3 48	..	..	9 3	..		..
58¼	Beal	9 4	..	..	4 5	..	..	9 20	..		..
63¼	Scremerston....	9 13	..	..	4 15	..	..	9 30	..		..
65½	Tweedmouth ..	9 20	11 43	..	4 23	..	..	9 38	..		..
66¾	**Berwick**..arr.	9 30	11 45	..	4 25	..	7 30	9 40	..		2 0
124¾	**Edinburgh**..	12 15	2 5	..	7 10	.	9 10	..	..	..	4 55
172¼	**Glasgow**	2 30	5 30	..	..	..	11 45	..	..	..	9 30

Station						Berwick to Edinbro', see page 72.			s. d.	s. d.	s. d.
Sunderland	..	8 35	9 0	..	7 35	9 50	..	..	16 6	13 10	9 0
Shields ..arr.	..	8 35	9 0	..	7 35	9 50	..	..	16 0	13 6	8 10
									FROM Newcastle		
Newcastle d	7 15	..	9 30	6 5	..		11 30	..	..	..	gov.
Killingworth	7 27	..	..	6 18	..		..	..	1 2	0 11	0 6
Cramlington	7 37	..	..	6 27	..		..	..	2 0	1 8	0 10
Netherton	7 47	..	..	6 37	..		..	..	2 9	2 0	1 2
Morpeth	7 55	..	10 5	6 46	..		.	..	3 0	2 3	1 5
Longhirst	8 4	..	..	6 54	..		..	..	4 0	3 4	1 8
Widdrington	8 12	..	..	7 7	..		..	..	4 3	3 10	1 11
Acklington	8 25	..	10 30	7 21	..		..	..	5 6	4 8	2 4
Warkworth	8 31	..	10 35	7 28	..		..	..	6 2	5 2	2 7
Lesbury, Alwk	8 41	..	10 45	7 39	..		..	..	7 0	5 10	2 11
Longhoughton	8 47	..	..	7 46	..		..	..	7 4	6 2	3 1
Christon Bank	9 4	..	..	8 1	..		..	..	8 6	7 2	3 7
Chathill	9 8	..	..	8 9	..		..	..	9 0	7 8	3 10
Lucker	9 16	..	..	8 18	..		..	..	9 8	8 2	4 1
Belford	9 22	..	11 15	8 23	..		..	..	10 0	8 6	4 3
Beal	9 40	..	..	8 40	..		..	..	11 6	9 8	4 10
Scremerston	9 50	.	..	8 50	..		..	..	12 6	10 6	5 3
Tweedmouth	9 58	..	11 43	8 58	..		..	..	13 0	11 0	5 6
Berwick..arr.	10 0	..	11 45	9 0	.		2 0	..	13 3	11 2	5 7
Edinburgh	..	..	2 5	..	..	..	4 55	..	..	..	..
Glasgow	..	..	..	..	..	..	..	..	..	..	..

DURHAM AND SUNDERLAND BRANCH.

SUNDERLAND TO DURHAM.

	a.m.	a.m.	p.m.	p.m.
Sunderland dep.	8 0	11 0	2 0	5 45
Murton	8 30	11 30	2 30	6 15
Hetton	8 40	11 40	2 40	6 25
Pittington	8 50	11 55	2 55	6 40
Sherburn, for Durham	9 0	12 6	3 0	6 50
Shincliffe	9 10	12 10	3 10	7 3

DURHAM TO SUNDERLAND.

	a.m.	a.m.	p.m.	p.m.
Durham (omnibus to Sherburn)..dep.	..	..	..	..
Shincliffe	7 45	10 45	1 45	5 30
Sherburn	7 50	10 50	1 50	5 35
Pittington	8 0	11 0	2 0	5 45
Hetton	8 10	11 10	2 10	6 0
Murton	8 20	11 20	2 20	6 10
Sunderland	8 50	11 50	2 50	6 40

SUNDERLAND TO HARTLEPOOL.

Sunderland..dep.	8 0	..	2 0	5 0
Haswell	8 50	..	2 50	5 50
Hartlepool.. arr.	9 25	..	3 25	6 25

HARTLEPOOL TO SUNDERLAND.

Hartlepool..dep.	8 15	..	2 15	5 15
Haswell	8 50	..	2 50	5 50
Sunderland..arr.	9 40	..	3 40	6 40

NEWCASTLE, SUNDERLAND AND SHIELDS.

WEEK DAYS.—Morning—5½, 8, 9, 10, 11 & 12.
Afternoon—1, 2, 3, 4, 5, 6, 7, 8 & 9.

SUNDAYS.—Morning—8 and 9½.
Afternoon—1, 2, 5½, 7 and 9.

FARES.—Newcastle to Sunderland, 1st class, 1s. 6d.; 2nd class, 1s. 3d.; 3rd class, 1s.; to Shields, 9d., 6d., and 4d.; Sunderland to Shields, 10d., 8d., and 6d.

SPRINGWELL AND JARROW TRAINS.

WEEK DAYS.—Morning—8 and 10.
Afternoon—2, 5 and 7.

SUNDAYS.—Morning—9½.
Afternoon—1, 5½, and 7.

An early timetable showing trains stopping at Lesbury

19. This was the first station for Alnwick but it closed when Bilton was opened. The station buildings were on the Down side and have the family likeness of the N&BR stations in its Gothic Tudor/Jacobean style (Jacobethan). Queen Victoria visited the station on 29th August 1850 on her way to open the Royal Border Bridge at Berwick. (J.M.Fleming)

20. This is a wider viewpoint but in the same northerly direction taken in February 1953. After closure it was converted into two railway cottages. When sold by BR about 1960, it was converted back to a single dwelling. (J.W.Armstrong/ARPT)

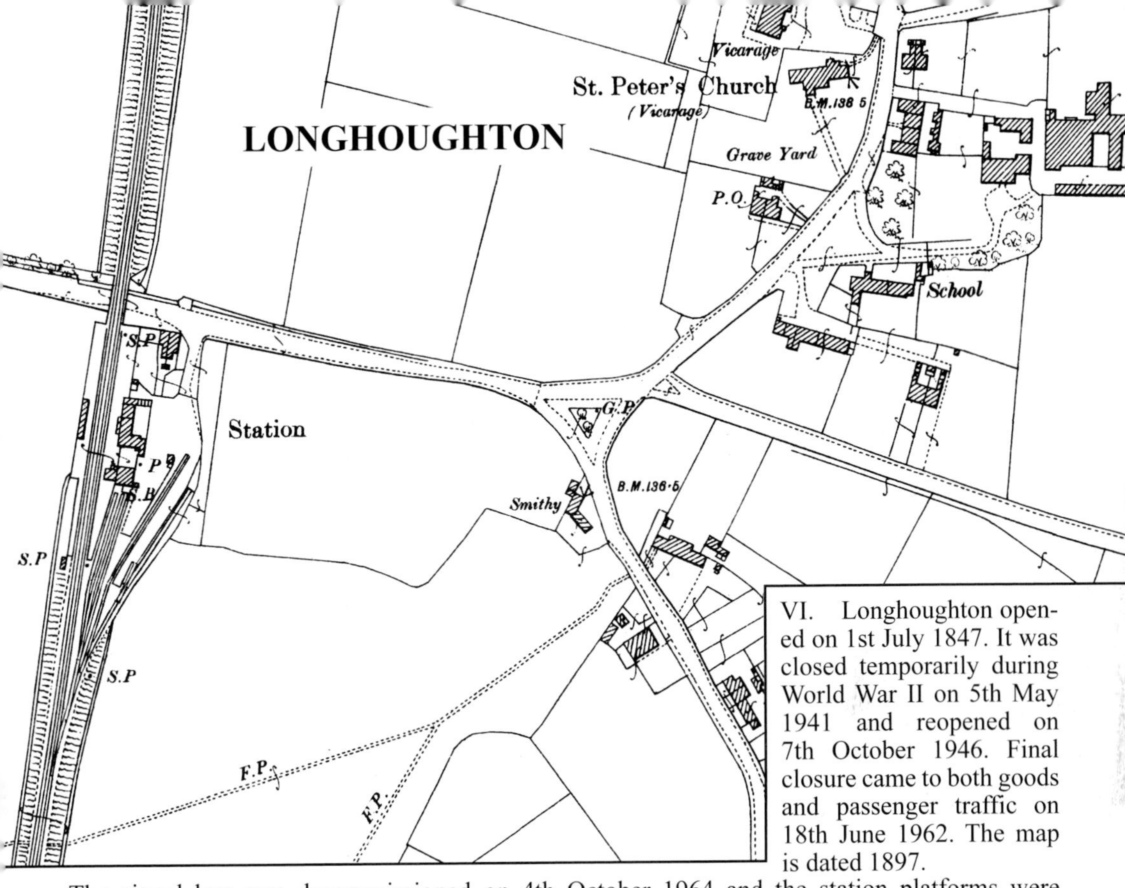

VI. Longhoughton opened on 1st July 1847. It was closed temporarily during World War II on 5th May 1941 and reopened on 7th October 1946. Final closure came to both goods and passenger traffic on 18th June 1962. The map is dated 1897.

The signal box was decommissioned on 4th October 1964 and the station platforms were demolished, the goods dock lasting to the early 1970s. The station cottages between the bridge and the station approach are in private hands. The Aln Valley Railway took up residence in the goods yard in April 2000 to undertake restoration on rolling stock prior to moving to their base at Lionheart on the outskirts of Alnwick 10 years later.

21. Benjamin Green's 'Jacobethan' style station was adapted here to serve platforms on an embankment. What appeared as a single storey from the platform was in fact two with offices and waiting rooms at platform height and living quarters down below. The goods shed dominated the Up platform, being a storey higher than the station at platform level. It was designed to complement the station's architecture. (J.F.Mallon/NERA)

22. The rear view of the station shows how imposing it was. The goods sidings were to the south and east of the station. The principal freight was whinstone, roadstone and livestock. The whinstone came from quarries at Ratcheugh and Longhoughton. Longhoughton quarry produced lime as well. (J.F.Mallon/NERA)

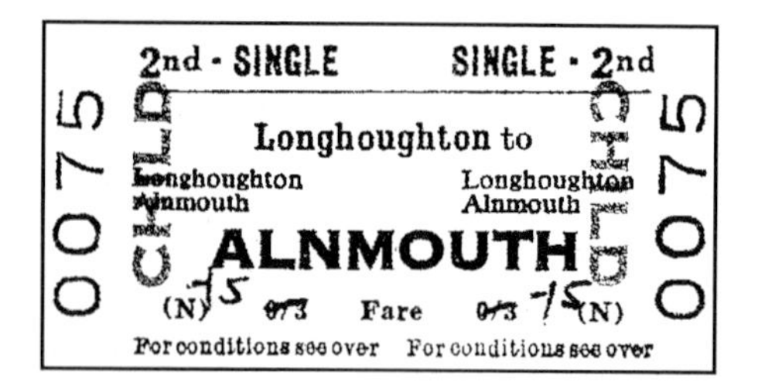

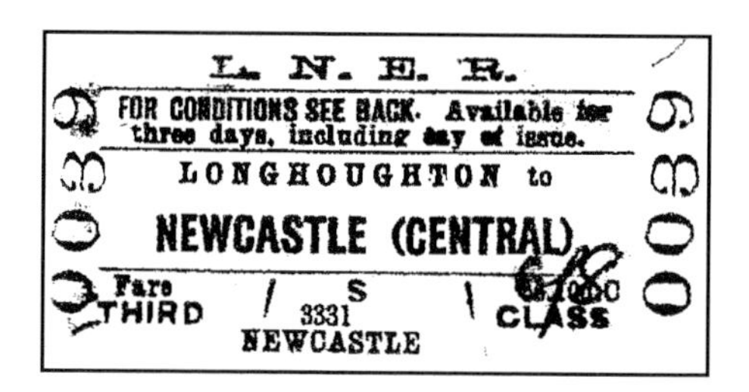

23. The sidings have Class D20 4-4-0 no. 62352 shunting wagons with the local pick-up goods train. The signal box was the second on the site. Built in 1909 with a 25 lever frame it lasted until 1960. The locomotive was withdrawn in June 1954. (J.F.Mallon/NERA)

SOUTH OF LITTLE MILL

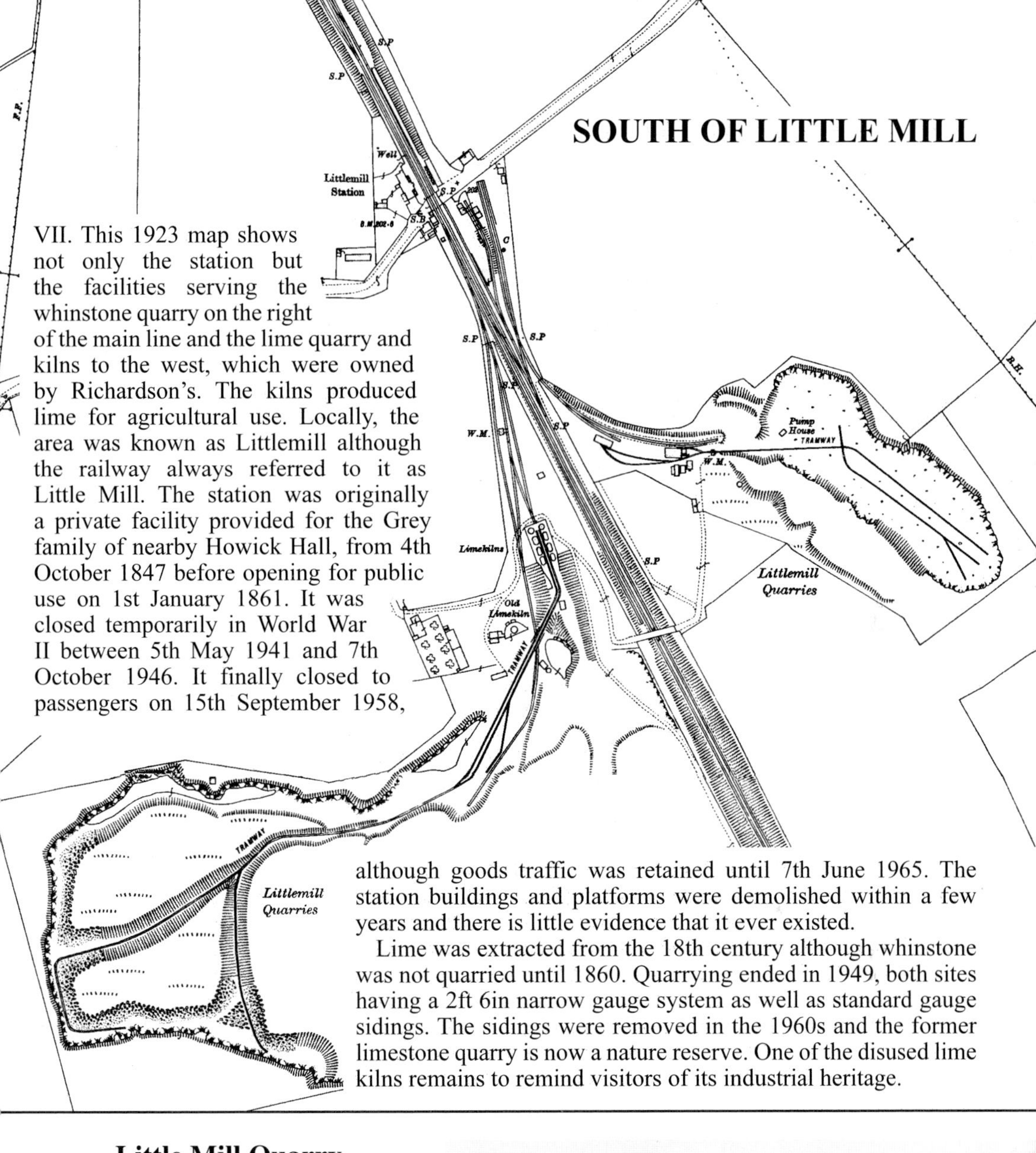

VII. This 1923 map shows not only the station but the facilities serving the whinstone quarry on the right of the main line and the lime quarry and kilns to the west, which were owned by Richardson's. The kilns produced lime for agricultural use. Locally, the area was known as Littlemill although the railway always referred to it as Little Mill. The station was originally a private facility provided for the Grey family of nearby Howick Hall, from 4th October 1847 before opening for public use on 1st January 1861. It was closed temporarily in World War II between 5th May 1941 and 7th October 1946. It finally closed to passengers on 15th September 1958, although goods traffic was retained until 7th June 1965. The station buildings and platforms were demolished within a few years and there is little evidence that it ever existed.

Lime was extracted from the 18th century although whinstone was not quarried until 1860. Quarrying ended in 1949, both sites having a 2ft 6in narrow gauge system as well as standard gauge sidings. The sidings were removed in the 1960s and the former limestone quarry is now a nature reserve. One of the disused lime kilns remains to remind visitors of its industrial heritage.

Little Mill Quarry

24. John H. Richardson had both narrow gauge and standard gauge systems at these quarries. This is the standard gauge locomotive 0-4-0ST *Despatch* (Manning Wardle 1230 of 1892). This came from Carr's Biscuit Co., Carlisle. The narrow gauge engine was 0-4-0ST Hunslet 268 of 1881. This was unusual as it had outside frames. Both locos mouldered away in the last days of the quarry, finally being scrapped in February 1951. (Lens of Sutton Association. LOSA)

LITTLE MILL

25. This original was a tinted postcard produced in September 1908. The main buildings were on the Down side. This was built as a private station for Earl Grey and his family, and there was originally no platform on the Up line. If Earl Grey summoned an Up train it crossed over to the Down platform. This practice continued for some years after the Up platform had been constructed. When the station was opened to the public, the facilities for passengers were on the Up side. Those on the Down side remained private. (J.Alsop coll.)

26. Here, we have a closer view of the main buildings on 16th July 1953. As might be expected, Queen Victoria alighted here, this time on 27th September 1849 while travelling south to open the High Level Bridge in Newcastle upon Tyne. (J.F.Mallon/NERA)

27. This features the crossing gates and the Up platform buildings and, again, the details are interesting; the wicker baskets – and look how enormous the awning supports are. Were they left over from something else? (J.F.Mallon/NERA)

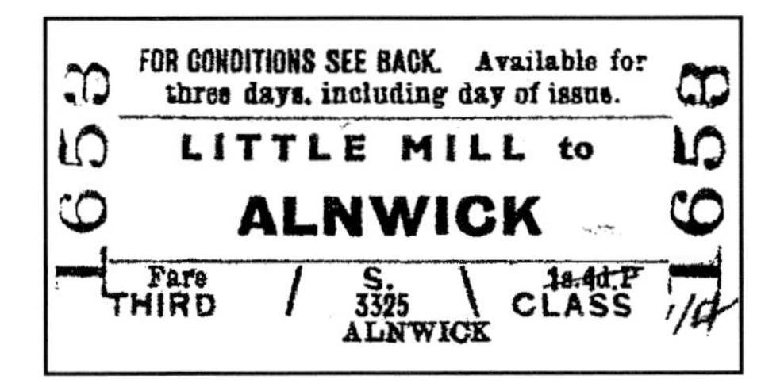

28. Class K1 2-6-0 no. 62030 is passing through with a very short pick-up goods, according to the lamp code. One van cannot be economic? No. 62030 was built in August 1949 to an A.H.Peppercorn design and lasted until August 1965. The signal box closed on 16th April 1978. (M.Halbert coll.)

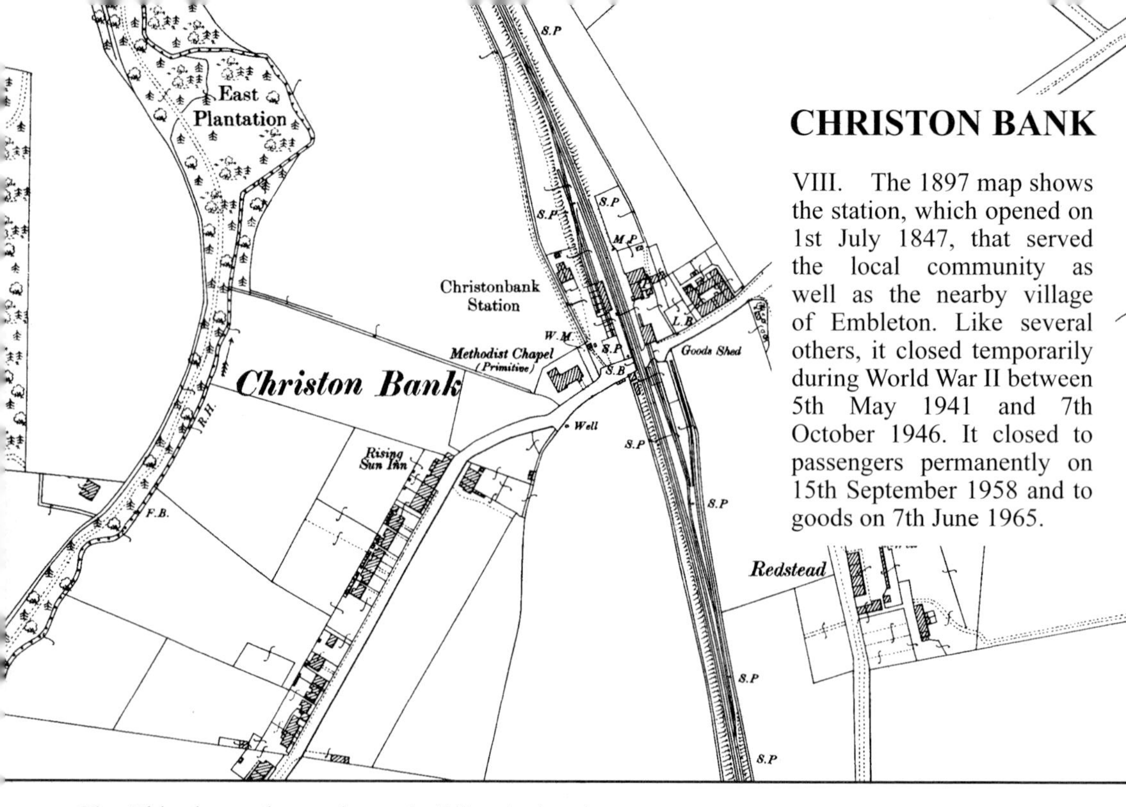

CHRISTON BANK

VIII. The 1897 map shows the station, which opened on 1st July 1847, that served the local community as well as the nearby village of Embleton. Like several others, it closed temporarily during World War II between 5th May 1941 and 7th October 1946. It closed to passengers permanently on 15th September 1958 and to goods on 7th June 1965.

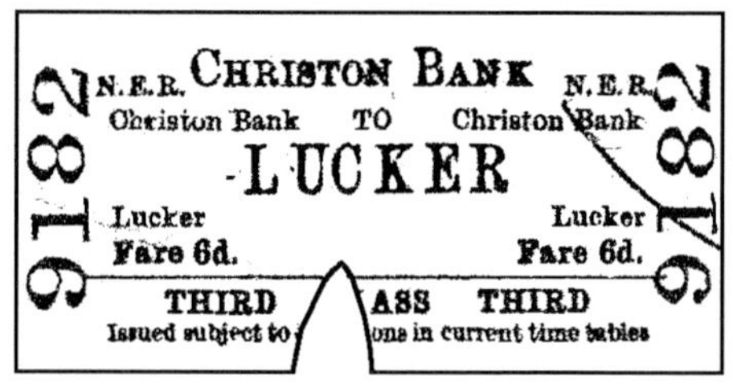

29. This shows the sandstone building in its glory in about 1910. Normally it would be milk churns on the platform, but these look more like beer barrels; although it has been suggested that they could contain fish. Local trains often picked up lamp oil and even water for isolated signal boxes. The main buildings are on the Up platform with coal drops to the west and the rest of the goods yard on the east, south of the level crossing. (J.Alsop coll.)

30. Looking south, this shows the relationship of the station, yard and signal box. The signal box dated from October 1877. It was an NER N2 design. In 1890 it had a Stevens frame with 24 levers, extended in 1912 to 35. (M.Halbert coll.)

L. N. E. R.	L. N. E. R.
MONTHLY RETURN	MONTHLY RETURN
LITTLE MILL	CHRISTON BANK
TO	TO
CHRISTON BANK	LITTLE MILL
Available for one month from date of issue	Available for one month from date of issue
Fare	Fare
THIRD	THIRD
For Conditions see back	For Conditions see back

0040 M.R. 3102 LITTLE MILL 0040

31. This was inside the signal box in 1958. It was a very traditional box, complete with hand wheel to operate the crossing gates. Besides the main line, the crossing gates also covered the siding to the goods shed. (K.Groundwater/ARPT)

32. A Deltic Co-CoDE in two-tone green livery was hauling passenger train 1A23. The platforms have been removed but there is still some business for the coal drops. The loco is said to be no. D9021 but the nameplate looks a bit short for *Argyll and Sutherland Highlander*. Both the station building and the goods shed are currently private dwellings. (Colour-Rail.com)

1939 Down Timetable

Table 157. NEWCASTLE, MORPETH, ALNMOUTH, BERWICK, DUNBAR AND EDINBURGH.

WEEKDAYS

Station (Table)										
	pm	pm	pm	pm	pm	pm	am			
LONDON (King's X) dep (103)	7c25	7c40	....	8c25	10c35	10c45	1 5			
York ,, (103)	11c16	11c31	11f50	1a11	2a55	3a17	4 55			
Darlington ,, (103)	10d44			2 13	3 8	4 14	5 48			
			MX							X
	am	am	am	am	am	am	am		am	am
	"THE HIGHLANDMAN"	"THE ABERDONIAN"					Restaurant Car		From Alnwick (dep 7-29 am)	
NEWCASTLE Central dep	1 0	1 15	1 34	3 15	4 45	6 13	7 0			
Manors East ,,										
Heaton ,,						6 18				
Forest Hall ,,						6 25				
Killingworth ,,						6 28				
Annitsford ,,						6 33				
Cramlington ,,						6 39				
Plessey ,,										
Stannington ,,						6 46				
Morpeth arr				3 41		6 51				
Morpeth dep				3 43		6 54				
Pegswood ,,										
Longhirst ,,						7 0				
Widdrington ,,						7 6				
Chevington ,,						7 12				
Acklington ,,						7 18				
Warkworth ,,						7 24				
Alnmouth arr				4 7		7 29	7 44		7 35	
Alnmouth dep				4 9			7 45		7 50	
Longhoughton ,,										
Little Mill ,,										
Christon Bank ,,									8 3	
Chathill ,,									8 9	
Newham ,,										
Lucker ,,									8 15	
Belford ,,									8 23	
Beal ,,									8 33	
Goswick ,,									8 38	
Scremerston ,,									8 44	
Tweedmouth ,, (B)									8 49	8 59
Berwick arr (B)				4 48	6 10		8 21			9 2
Berwick dep				4 54	6 12		8 23			
Dunbar arr (A)					8k10		8 59			
Drem ,, (A)					7g 1		10n57			
EDINBURGH (Waverley) ,, (A)	3 35	3 50	4 0	6 6	7 30		9 36			

Station (Table)									
	K							K	
				am				am	am
LONDON (King's X) dep (103)								4 45	4 45
York ,, (103)								9 30	9 38
Darlington ,, (103)				8 35				9 57	9 57
	am	am		am		am	am	am	am
	Buffet Car			Buffet Car			To Alnwick (arr 11-37 am)	Buffet Car	Restaurant Car
NEWCASTLE Central dep	7 40	8 15		9 32			10 8	11 2	1110
Manors East ,,		8 17					1010		
Heaton ,,		8 21					1014		
Forest Hall ,,		8 28					1021		
Killingworth ,,		8 31					1024		
Annitsford ,,		8 36					1029		
Cramlington ,,		8 42					1035		
Plessey ,,		8 46					1039		
Stannington ,,		8 51					1044		
Morpeth arr	8 5	8 57		9 57			1049		
Morpeth dep	8 7	9 4		9 59			1050		
Pegswood ,,		9 9					1054		
Longhirst ,,		9 13					1058		
Widdrington ,,		9 21					11 4		
Chevington ,,		9 28					1110		
Acklington ,,		9 37					1116		
Warkworth ,,		9 44					1122		
Alnmouth arr	8 30	9 50		1022			1127		
Alnmouth dep	8 32	9 58		1024			1130		
Longhoughton ,,		10 4							
Little Mill ,,		10 9							
Christon Bank ,,		1015							
Chathill ,,		1024		1040					
Newham ,,		1028							
Lucker ,,		1033							
Belford ,,	8 56	1038		1050		11 0			
Beal ,,				11 0		1111			
Goswick ,,						1116			
Scremerston ,,						1122			
Tweedmouth ,, (B)						1131			
Berwick arr (B)	9 15			1113		1134			
Berwick dep	9 18			1117					
Dunbar arr (A)	9 54			1155					
Drem ,, (A)	10e25			1211					
EDINBURGH (Waverley) ,, (A)	10 33			1238				1 27	1 35

Station (Table)									
			SX	SO	SO	SX	N	C	
		am					am	am	
LONDON (King's X) dep (103)									7
York ,, (103)		10 5					1050	1120	11
Darlington ,, (103)		11 7					1144	12p11	12
	am	pm	pm	pm	pm	pm	pm	pm	
	To Alnwick (arr 12-44 pm)						Restaurant Car	Buffet Car	
NEWCASTLE Central dep	1123	1212			1223	1238	1242	1 5	1
Manors East ,,	1125				1225	1240			
Heaton ,,	1129				1229	1244			
Forest Hall ,,	1136				1236	1251			
Killingworth ,,	1139				1239	1254			
Annitsford ,,	1144				1244	1259			
Cramlington ,,	1150				1259	1 5			
Plessey ,,					1 3	1 9			
Stannington ,,					1 8	1 14			
Morpeth arr	12 2	1237			1 13	1 19			
Morpeth dep	12 4	1239							
Pegswood ,,									
Longhirst ,,									
Widdrington ,,	1214								
Chevington ,,									
Acklington ,,	1224								
Warkworth ,,	1230								
Alnmouth arr	1235	1 2							
Alnmouth dep	1237	1 5	1 15	1 37					
Longhoughton ,,			1 21	1 43					
Little Mill ,,			1 26	2h11					
Christon Bank ,,			1 32	2 17					
Chathill ,,		1 22	1 38	2 23					
Newham ,,			1 41	2 26					
Lucker ,,			1 46	2 31					
Belford ,,		1 32	1 51	2 36					
Beal ,,			2 1	2 46					
Goswick ,,			2 6	2 51					
Scremerston ,,			2 12	2 57					
Tweedmouth ,, (B)			2 19	3 4					
Berwick arr (B)		1 51	2 22	3 7			2 2	2 25	2
Berwick dep							2 5	2 27	2
Dunbar arr (A)							2 41	3 2	3
Drem ,, (A)									4
EDINBURGH (Waverley) ,, (A)							3 21	3 40	3

A For complete service between Berwick and Edinburgh see Scottish Area Time Table.
B For other trains between Tweedmouth and Berwick see Table 168.
C Saturdays only. Runs 22nd July to 19th August inclusive.
K Saturdays only and not after 2nd September.
MX Mondays excepted.
N Saturdays only and not after 9th September.

SO Saturdays only.
SX Saturdays excepted.
X One class only.
a am.
c Also applies on Sunday nights.
d On Sunday nights leaves 10-33 pm.
e Change at Dunbar.
f Sunday nights excepted.

g On Saturdays until 16th September inclusive calls at Drem to set down passengers from King's Cross. On other days calls when required to set down passengers from King's Cross.
h Arrives Little Mill 1-48 pm.
j On Saturdays leaves King's Cross 7-30 am.
k Change at Berwick.
n Change at Dunbar. On Saturdays arrives 10-25 am.
p pm.

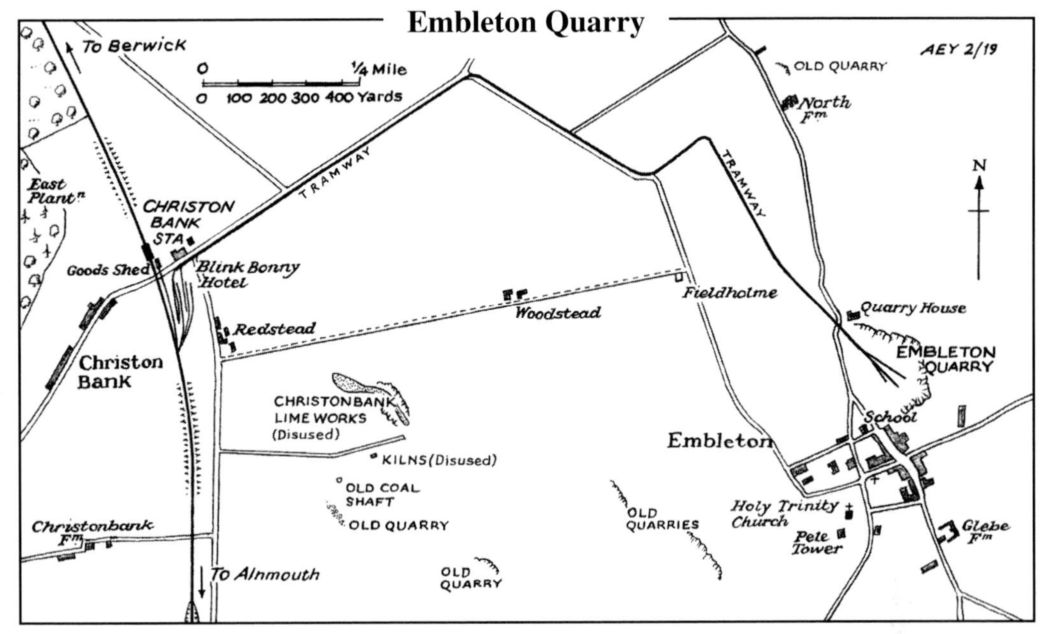

IX. A whinstone quarry was opened by the Appleby family in the 1860s and, at its peak, it employed up to 80 people. It provided setts, chippings and building stones, and the Mersey Tunnel is paved with setts from the quarry. The line was served by a 2ft 9in gauge tramway that was operated by two German-built steam locomotives. It ran to exchange facilities with the standard gauge sidings at Christon Bank goods yard. Most of the line ran alongside local roads. The quarry closed in 1963, although the last blasting had taken place in January 1962. The quarry was later used for landfill by Northumberland County Council, until the 1990s when it became a wildlife haven. (A.E.Young)

33. This is a posed photo at the Appleby's quarry, but it does show the two locomotives that operated the narrow gauge line to Christon Bank. *Fanny Gray* 0-4-0WT, in the foreground, was Orenstein & Koppel 3248 of 1909 and *Dunstanburgh* 0-4-0WT was Jung 812 of 1904. The railway was horse-drawn from 1898, with steam power from 1904. It ran until 1941 but the locos were not scrapped until 1955. (Northumberland Gazette/R.Jermy coll.)

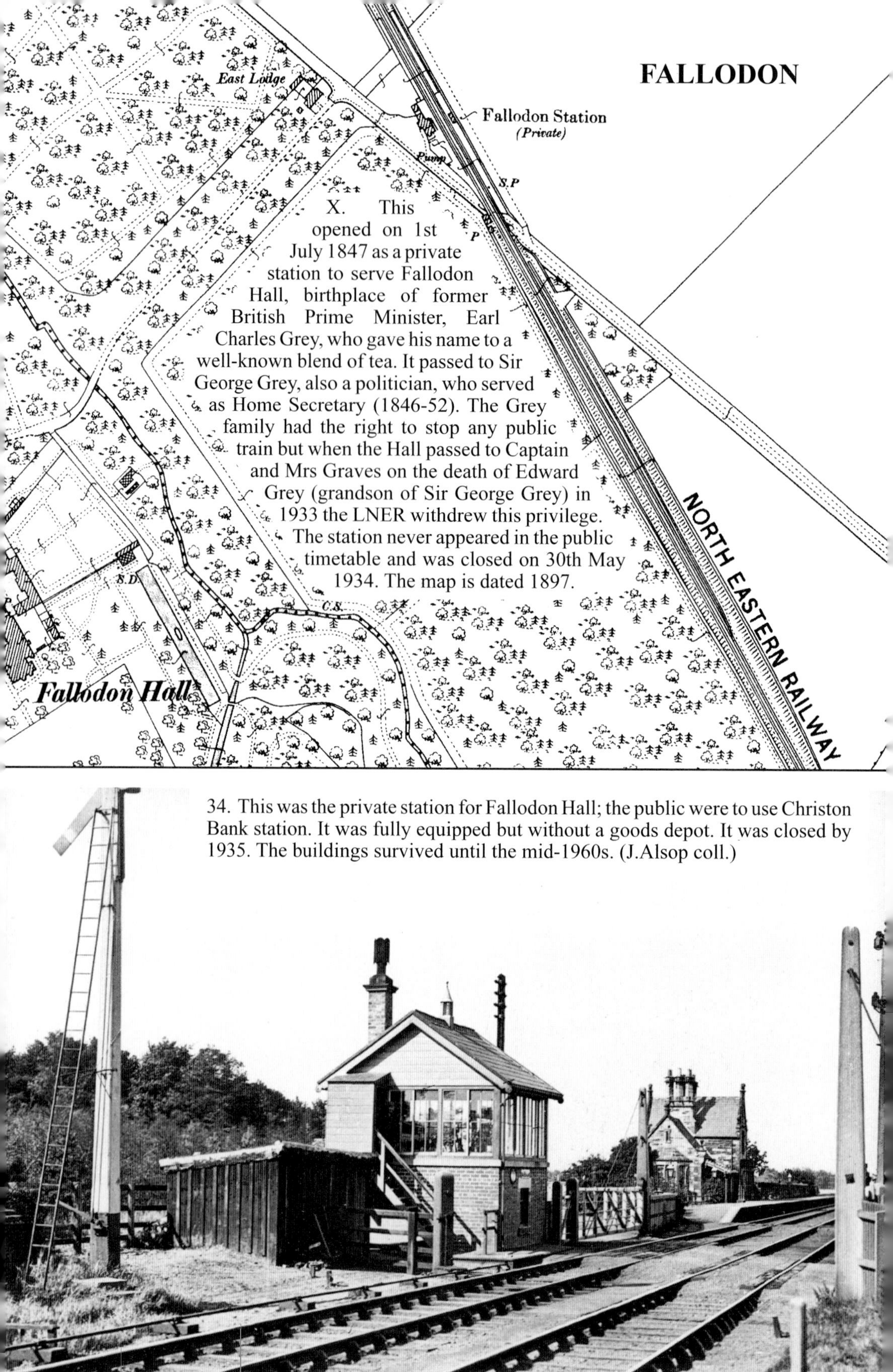

X. This opened on 1st July 1847 as a private station to serve Fallodon Hall, birthplace of former British Prime Minister, Earl Charles Grey, who gave his name to a well-known blend of tea. It passed to Sir George Grey, also a politician, who served as Home Secretary (1846-52). The Grey family had the right to stop any public train but when the Hall passed to Captain and Mrs Graves on the death of Edward Grey (grandson of Sir George Grey) in 1933 the LNER withdrew this privilege. The station never appeared in the public timetable and was closed on 30th May 1934. The map is dated 1897.

34. This was the private station for Fallodon Hall; the public were to use Christon Bank station. It was fully equipped but without a goods depot. It was closed by 1935. The buildings survived until the mid-1960s. (J.Alsop coll.)

35. The building looked impressive from the roadside. An Austin A30 gives the approximate date of the photograph as the 1950s. The railway never made a profit from the station, but it was a shame that having lasted so long it wasn't kept as a private dwelling. (E.E.Smith/ARPT)

36. In 1958, the station was long closed but still intact. Class K3 2-6-0 no. 61928 comes through with an express freight 'with at least four fitted vehicles connected to the loco'. The engine was built by Armstrong Whitworth in 1934 and was withdrawn in February 1960. Originally allocated to Gateshead, this locomotive worked out of St. Margaret's, Edinburgh, from 1949. (E.E.Smith/ARPT)

CHATHILL

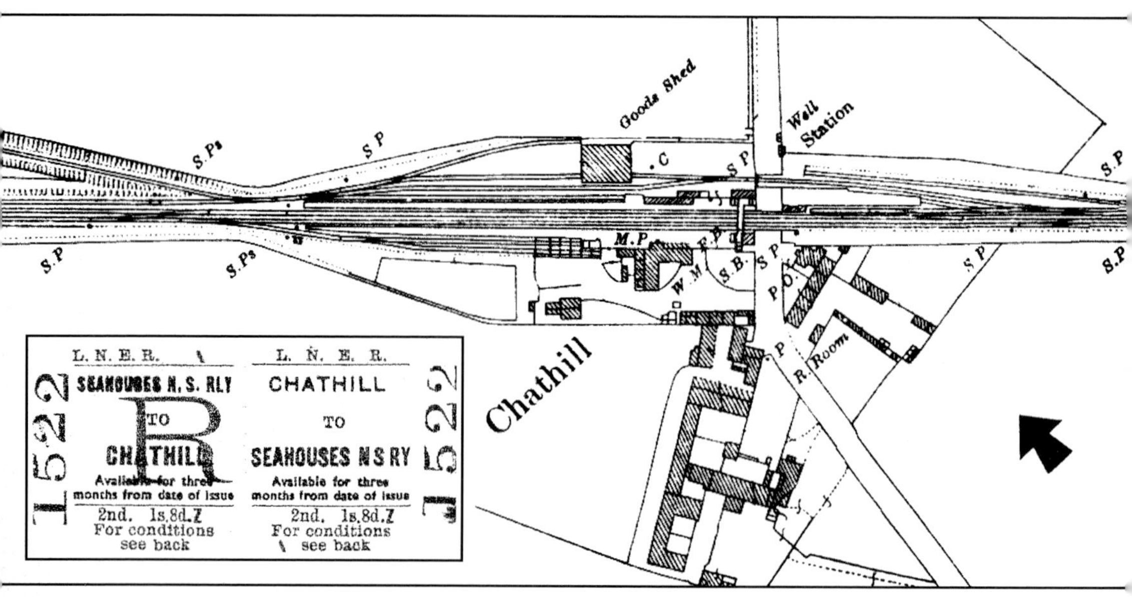

XI. Opened on 29th March 1847, this is one of the few stations between Newcastle and Berwick to remain open, albeit with a very limited service of two trains per day provided by Northern. This 1922 map shows the extensive facilities for the junction station that served the North Sunderland branch to Seahouses from the following year. The goods yard remained until closure on 7th June 1965.

37. This is another of Benjamin Green's fine designs. The main buildings are on the Down line. From 1898 to 1951 the station carried 'Chathill for Seahouses' on its platform signs. It was the junction for the North Sunderland Railway and, in 2020, there was still a signal board labelled 'Chathill Junction'. On 28th July 1977, a blue Deltic with blue and grey coaches was going north. (A.E.Young)

38. We are looking north under the wires. The station is still open though the building is now a private house. For some time the owner decorated the outside with a collection of signs in the orange colour of the British Railways North Eastern Region. This photograph was taken from the level crossing on 25th June 2013. (D.A.Lovett)

39. This was the 2A40 train from Carlisle (dep. 16.23) to Chathill via Newcastle (arr. 18.51). It was DMU no. 156472, seen here on Bank Holiday Monday, 26th August 2019. (M.T.Snowball)

40. It is the same Bank Holiday Monday and LNER Hitachi ‘Azuma’ class 800/1 no. 800107 is heading through Chathill, towards Morpeth, with the 1E23 10.30 Edinburgh to Kings Cross. (M.T.Snowball)

NORTH SUNDERLAND RAILWAY

41. 0-4-0DE Armstrong Whitworth D25 of 1934, named *The Lady Armstrong*, comes off the NSR line into the sidings at Chathill. The single coach was normal except for the summer high season when three coaches were needed. The diesel was an early class, two of which survive in preservation. (ARPT)

42. Y7 class 0-4-0T no. 68089 and driver wait at Chathill to leave for Seahouses. Possibly there may be passengers from the train hauled by a class V2 2-6-2 entering the station. Notice the full station name board. (W.A.Camwell)

EAST OF CHATHILL

43. The NSR had a nicely uniform rake of ex-NER 4-wheel coaches with a birdcage brake van at the end. The year is 1926 and the locomotive is a class J79 0-6-0T no. 407. This loco stood in for the NSR's own locomotive *Bamburgh* from 11th August. The photograph was taken near East Fleetham. There was another J79, no. 1787, and it was loaned by the LNER in 1933 when *Bamburgh* was again out of service. Both J79s were withdrawn in 1935, with no. 407 going to a colliery at Castleford and no. 1787 to the Bowes Railway. (C.L.J.Romanes/M.Halbert coll.)

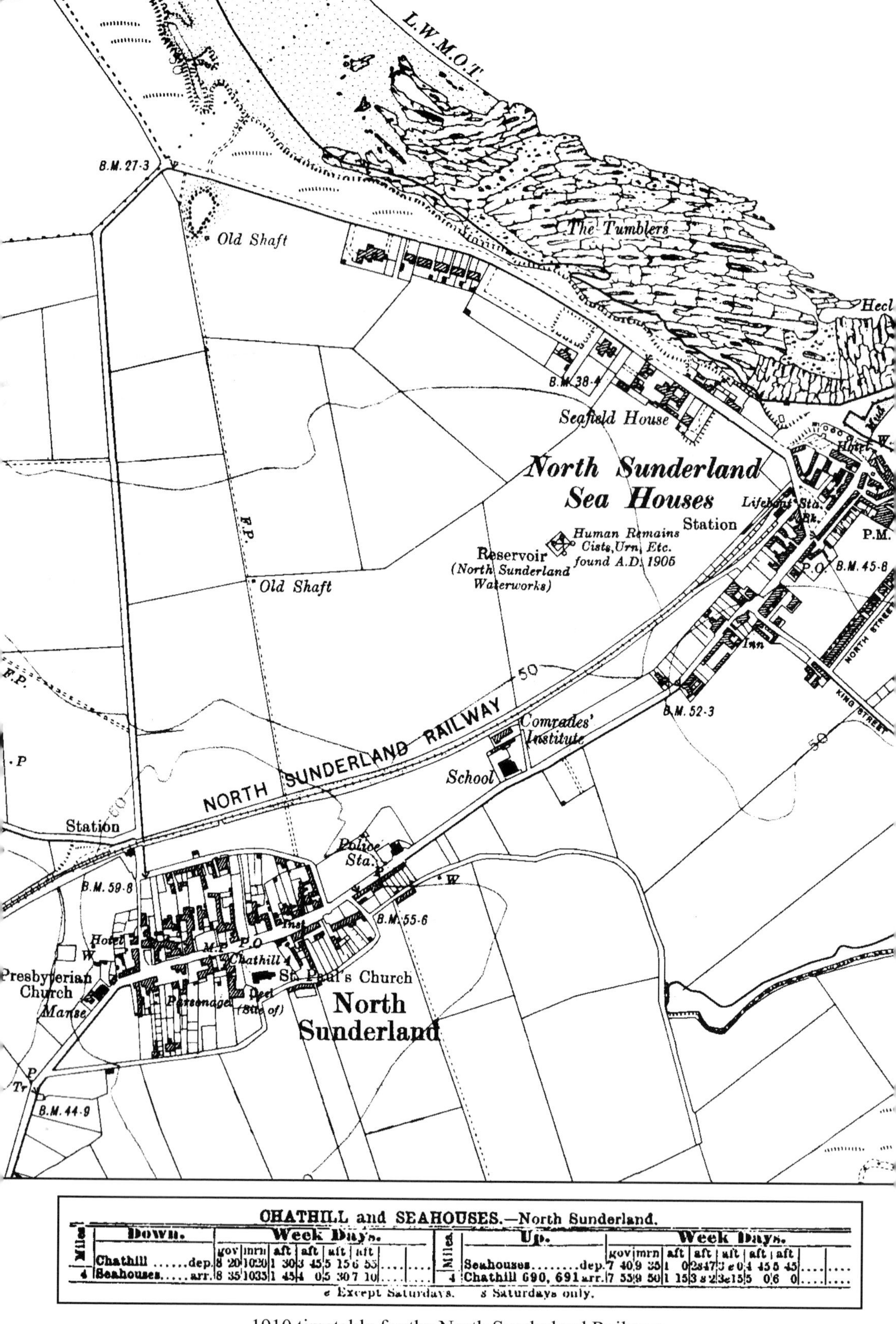

CHATHILL and SEAHOUSES.—North Sunderland.

Miles	Down.	Week Days.							
		gov	mrn	aft	aft	aft	aft		
	Chathill ......dep.	8 20	1020	1 30	3 45	5 15	6 55	....	....
4	Seahouses.....arr.	8 35	1035	1 45	4 0	5 30	7 10	....	....

Miles	Up.	Week Days.								
		gov	mrn	aft	aft	aft	aft	aft		
	Seahouses........dep.	7 40	9 35	1 0	2s47	3e0	4 45	5 45	....	....
4	Chathill 690, 691 arr.	7 55	9 50	1 15	3s2	3e15	5 0	6 0	....	....

e Except Saturdays. *s* Saturdays only.

1910 timetable for the North Sunderland Railway.

NORTH SUNDERLAND

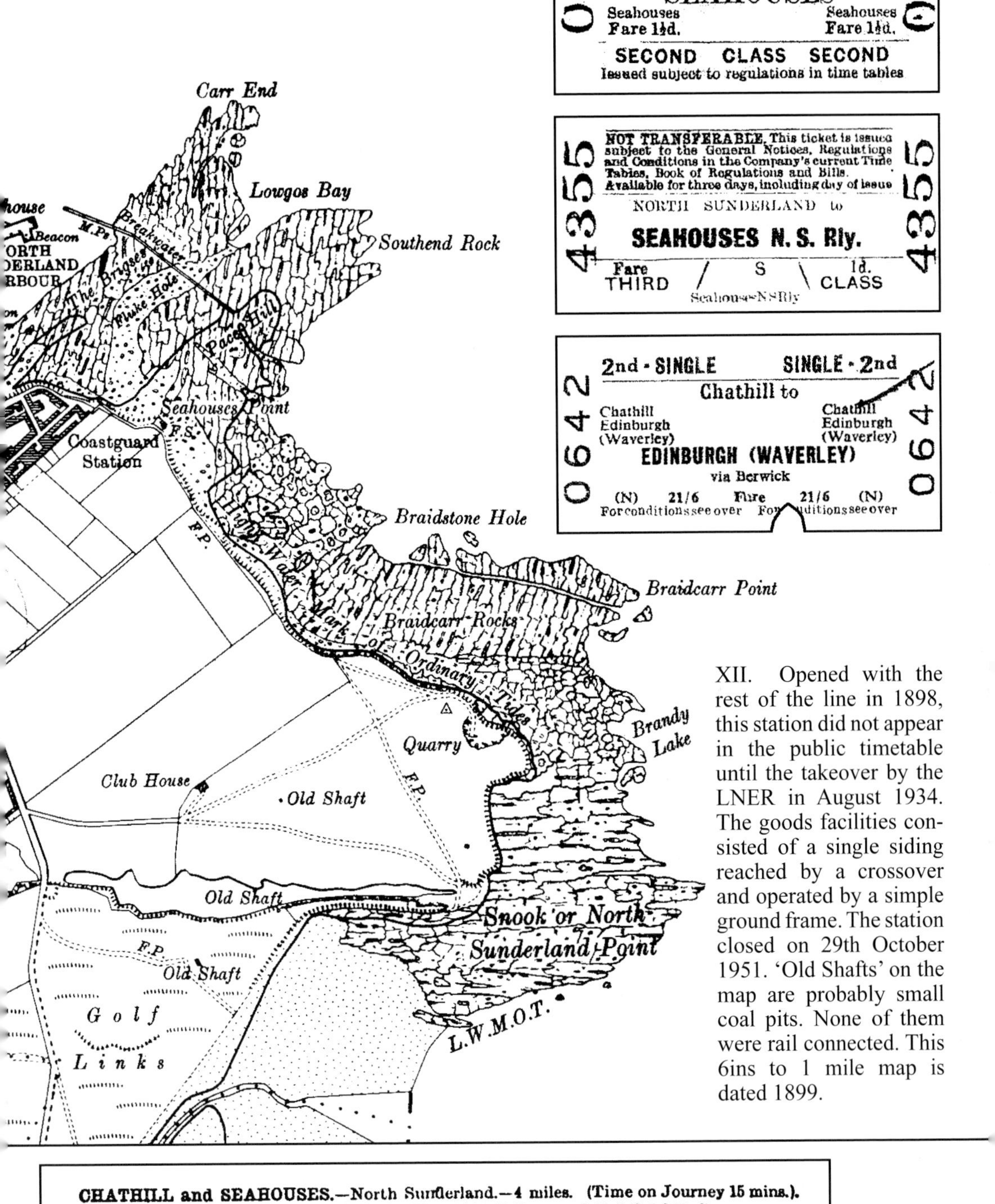

XII. Opened with the rest of the line in 1898, this station did not appear in the public timetable until the takeover by the LNER in August 1934. The goods facilities consisted of a single siding reached by a crossover and operated by a simple ground frame. The station closed on 29th October 1951. 'Old Shafts' on the map are probably small coal pits. None of them were rail connected. This 6ins to 1 mile map is dated 1899.

CHATHILL and SEAHOUSES.—North Sunderland.—4 miles. (Time on Journey 15 mins.).
Chathill to Seahouses. WEEK DAYS at 8 14 & 10 48 mrn. ; 1 45, 5 42. & 6 50 aft.
Trains call at North Sunderland 12 mins. after leaving Chathill.
Seahouses to Chathill. WEEK DAYS at 7 48 & 9 20 mrn. ; 1 0, 4 10, & 6 20 aft.
Trains call at North Sunderland 3 mins. after leaving Seahouses.

1938 version for the line.

44. The station buildings were off the east end of the platform. They consisted of a waiting room and the station master/crossing keeper's cottage. (E.E.Smith/M.Halbert coll.)

45. This was the station platform in the 1920s. The running-in board was lit by an oil lamp and the single advert was for Petter's oil engines. 0-6-0ST *Bamburgh* was under repair in the overgrown sidings. The locomotive was built in 1898 by Manning Wardle, their no. 1394. (H.C.Casserley/R.M.Casserley)

SEAHOUSES

46. The station opened on 14th December 1898; a proposed branch to Bamburgh from the terminus failed to get built. The station was located across the road from the harbour and consisted of a single platform, a small goods shed and a locomotive shed (see map XII on the previous page). The station closed on 29th October 1951. The station site today is a large car park for the popular seaside village. Boats leave from the harbour to visit the Farne Islands. Proposals to take the station sidings down to the pier never materialised. 0-4-0DE *The Lady Armstrong* is shown here with its train in happier days: flowers, fences and a locomotive in polished black livery lined with red. The railway even had a named train 'The Farne Islander'. Before the diesel locomotive was hired, the Armstrong Whitworth demonstrator diesel was tried out on the line. This was a 95 BHP 0-6-0DE D10 of 1932. (J.Alsop coll.)

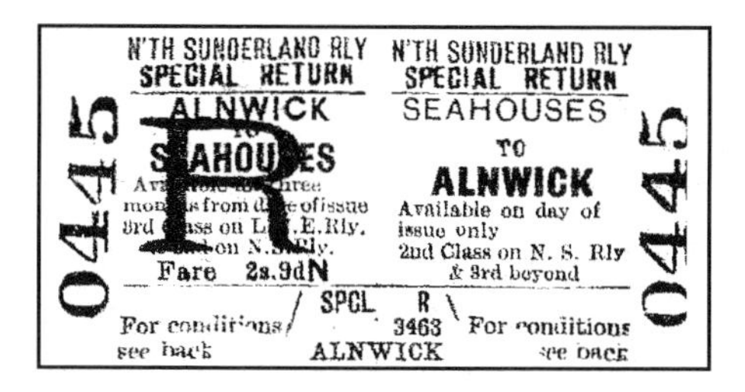

47. This classic photograph of the NSR was taken on 2nd October 1951. Class Y7 0-4-0T no. 68089, with its train and crew, poses in the station. In the background is the engine shed and one of the goods sheds. Note the mix of concrete and wooden sleepers on the track. (N.E.Stead coll./ Transport Library)

48. The railway often ran mixed trains. No. 68089 is on the front of the train that includes one fish van, a four-wheel composite coach and a four-wheel saloon converted to a brake van. A postman has brought the mail from the Post Office on an elegant barrow. Behind the train is the station and railway office. The date is 2nd October 1951. (N.E.Stead coll./Transport Library)

49. Sidings to the harbour would have been useful to save transhipment. As roads and lorries improved, so the cost of transhipment worked against the railway. BTY 316 is an Austin K2 lorry and the carriages are ex NER. (C.G.Raynes/R.Humm coll.)

The final schedules for the North Sunderland Railway as they appeared before closure in the British Railways North Eastern Region timetable for 1951.

CHATHILL and SEAHOUSES

(NORTH SUNDERLAND RAILWAY)

Table 75

WEEKDAYS									
		am	am	am	am	pm	pm	pm	
Edinburgh	dep	....	6 55	....	10 25	2 30	....	....	....
Berwick	,,	7 22	8 55	..	12p11	4 20	..	..	..
Newcastle	dep	....	7 15	9 28	12p21	4 18	6 5	....	....
		am	am	am	pm	pm	pm		
CHATHILL	dep	8 10	9 35	10 50	1 40	5 50	7 35	..	..
North Sunderland	,,	8 27	9 52	11 7	1 57	6 7	7 52	....	....
SEAHOUSES	arr	8 30	9 55	11 10	2 0	6 10	7 55	..	..

WEEKDAYS									
		am	am	am	pm	pm	pm		
SEAHOUSES	dep	7 35	8 55	10 5	12 15	4 20	6 45	....	....
North Sunderland	,,	7 38	8 58	10 8	12 18	4 23	6 48	..	..
CHATHILL	arr	7 55	9 15	10 25	12 35	4 40	7 5	....	....
		am	am	am	pm	pm	pm		
Newcastle	arr	9 29	10K45	..	2D0	6 11	11A10	..	..
Berwick	arr	....	10 7	11 7	2 8	6 25	8B3	....	....
Edinburgh	,,	..	..	12p41	3 35	9J2	10 0	..	..

A—On Saturdays arrives Newcastle 10.51 pm B—On Saturdays arrives Berwick 8.6 pm D—On Thursdays and Saturdays arrives Newcastle 2.3 pm J—On Saturdays arrives Edinburgh 9.4 pm K—On Saturdays arrives Newcastle 10.50 am p—pm

Full particulars of services in North Eastern England can be obtained on request at stations

Other communications regarding train services should be addressed to the District Passenger Superintendent, Newcastle

The train services shown here are subject to alteration or cancellation at short notice and do not necessarily apply at Bank and Public Holiday periods

BYE-LAWS AND REGULATIONS – GENERAL NOTICES, REGULATIONS AND CONDITIONS
Copies of the bye-laws and regulations will be found exhibited at stations

A booklet showing the conditions upon which tickets, including season tickets, are issued, and the regulations and conditions applicable to passengers' luggage, can be obtained, free of charge, from the station booking office.

NE 49

Seahouses Engine Shed

50. Class Y7 0-4-0T no. 68089 was sticking out of the shed. It was transferred from Tyne Dock on 14th November 1948 to Tweedmouth and withdrawn on 25th January 1952, when it went to Morecambe Harbour & General Works. Here, it carried the name *Eve*. Interestingly, when the Y7 went to Darlington Works a former Lancashire & Yorkshire Railway 'pug' no. 11207 was used on the branch. It arrived from Derby on 8th October and returned to Burton on 12th December 1948. (C.G.Raynes/R.Humm coll.)

51. This is an early picture of *Bamburgh* outside the shed. Its livery was a slightly darker green than that of NER, lined with broad black lines edged with white. After valiant service, the locomotive was scrapped on 11th October 1949. (ARPT)

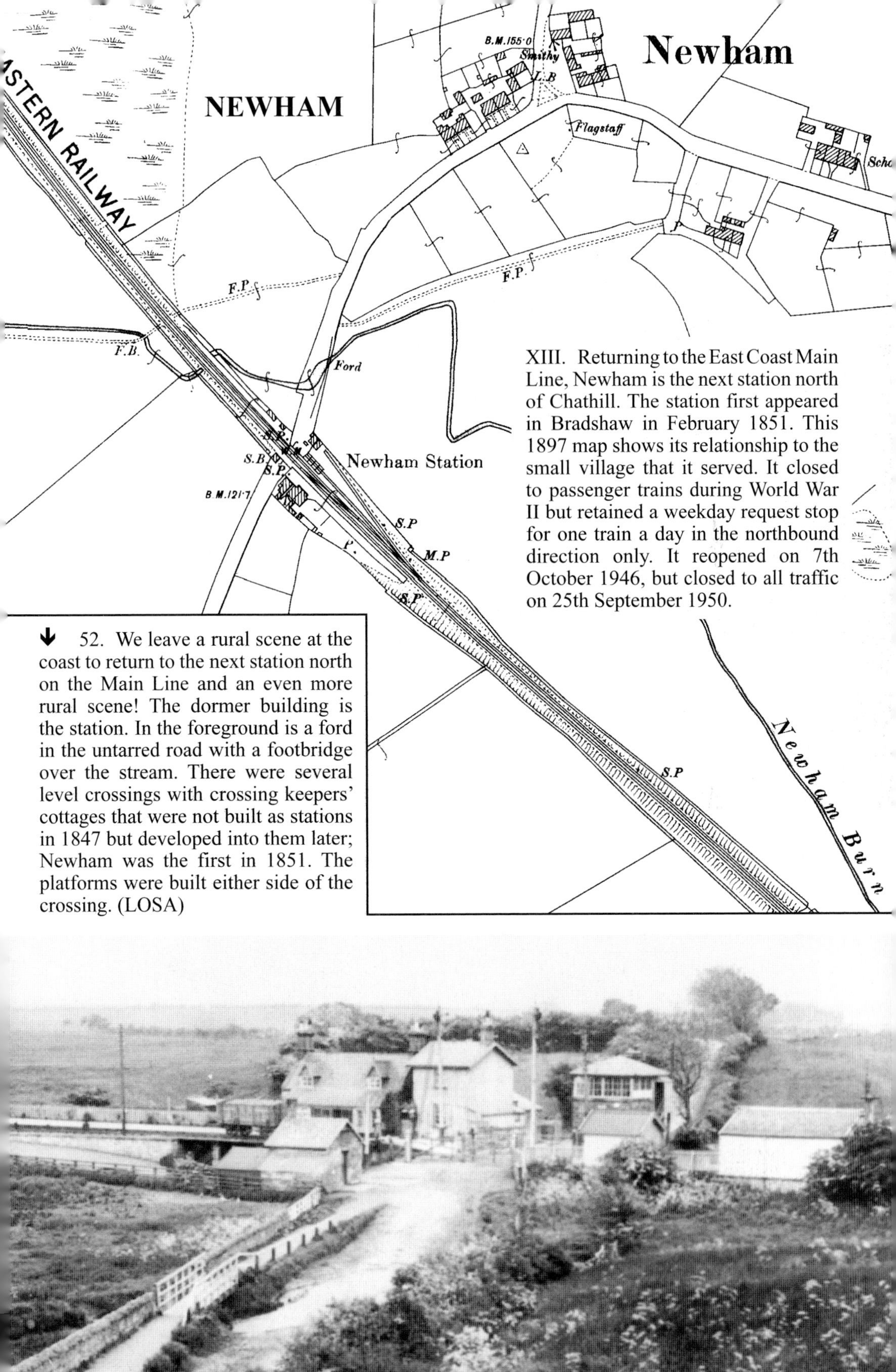

XIII. Returning to the East Coast Main Line, Newham is the next station north of Chathill. The station first appeared in Bradshaw in February 1851. This 1897 map shows its relationship to the small village that it served. It closed to passenger trains during World War II but retained a weekday request stop for one train a day in the northbound direction only. It reopened on 7th October 1946, but closed to all traffic on 25th September 1950.

↓ 52. We leave a rural scene at the coast to return to the next station north on the Main Line and an even more rural scene! The dormer building is the station. In the foreground is a ford in the untarred road with a footbridge over the stream. There were several level crossings with crossing keepers' cottages that were not built as stations in 1847 but developed into them later; Newham was the first in 1851. The platforms were built either side of the crossing. (LOSA)

53. The road is now tarred and the gates more substantial, though still hand-operated with a cabin for the gate keeper. The cans are probably for signal oil. The limited number of trains that stopped meant there was time for the station garden to be tended, providing its noted floral displays. (J.W.Armstrong/ARPT)

54. The platforms had gone by the early 1960s and in 1968 the buildings were private houses. The gate cabin still had the station name on the side. The station cottages survived until 1971 and, in 2001, the station house was replaced by a new bungalow on the site. (J.C.Dean/NERA)

LUCKER

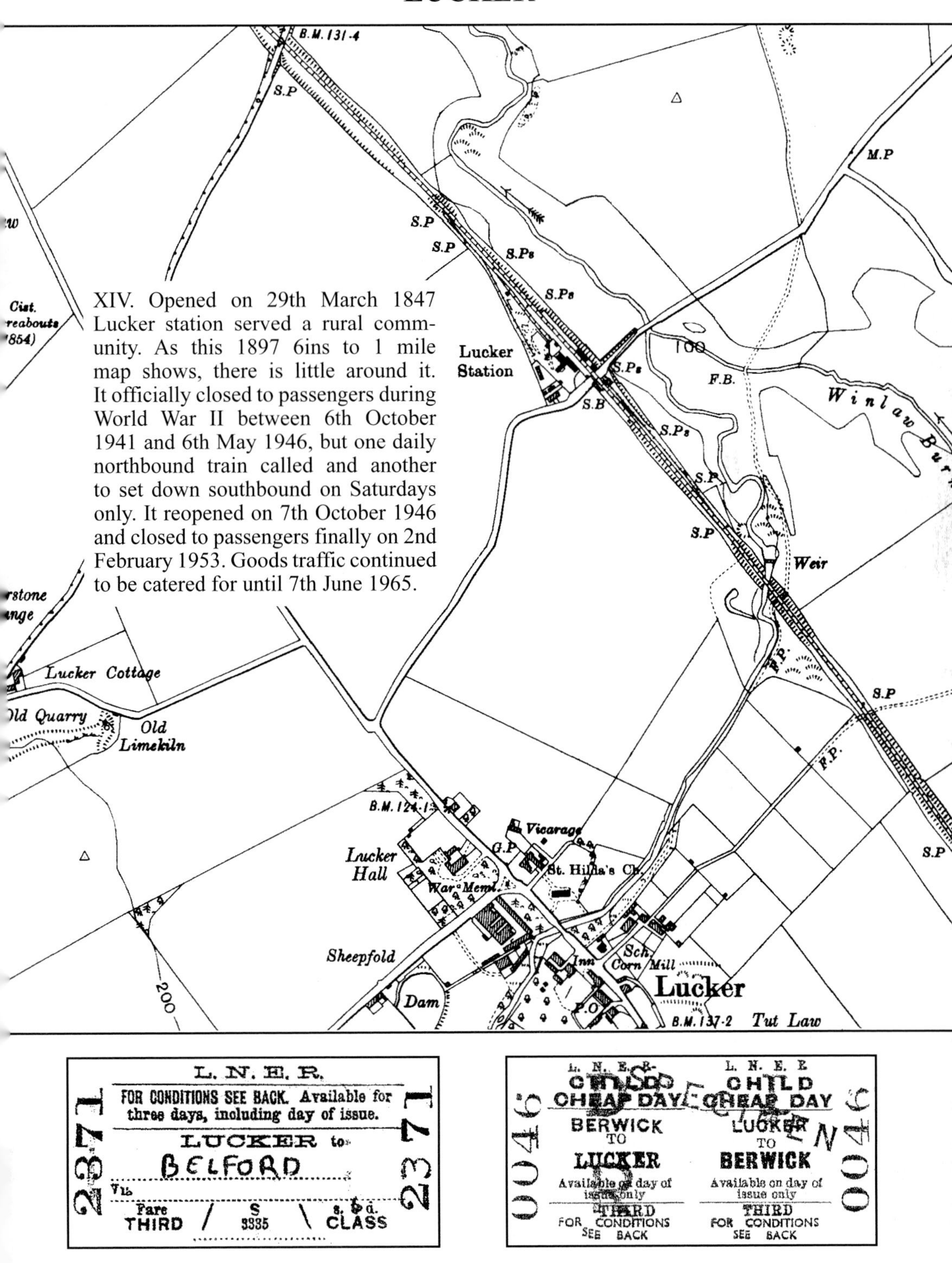

XIV. Opened on 29th March 1847 Lucker station served a rural community. As this 1897 6ins to 1 mile map shows, there is little around it. It officially closed to passengers during World War II between 6th October 1941 and 6th May 1946, but one daily northbound train called and another to set down southbound on Saturdays only. It reopened on 7th October 1946 and closed to passengers finally on 2nd February 1953. Goods traffic continued to be catered for until 7th June 1965.

55. A postcard from about 1908 shows one of the fine designs of the stations on this section of the line. The splendour of the building comes from a covenant between George Hudson and the Duke of Northumberland that Lucker and Warkworth would be 'First Class stations'. In service potential however it was one of the minor stations of the line. (J.Alsop coll.)

56. The building is still showing its magnificence although the platforms have been removed and piles of platform coping stones remain to be collected. Unfortunately, the whole building was demolished in the summer of 1960. (J.F.Mallon/NERA)

57. This photograph concentrates on the level crossing and signal box. A Ford Anglia waits as class V2 2-6-2 no. 60952, a Gateshead engine, comes past on a Down goods. The signal box was an NER N1 design, opened in 1873 and closed on 20th August 1978, to be replaced by CCTV at Chathill. (R.Humm coll.)

Lucker Water Troughs

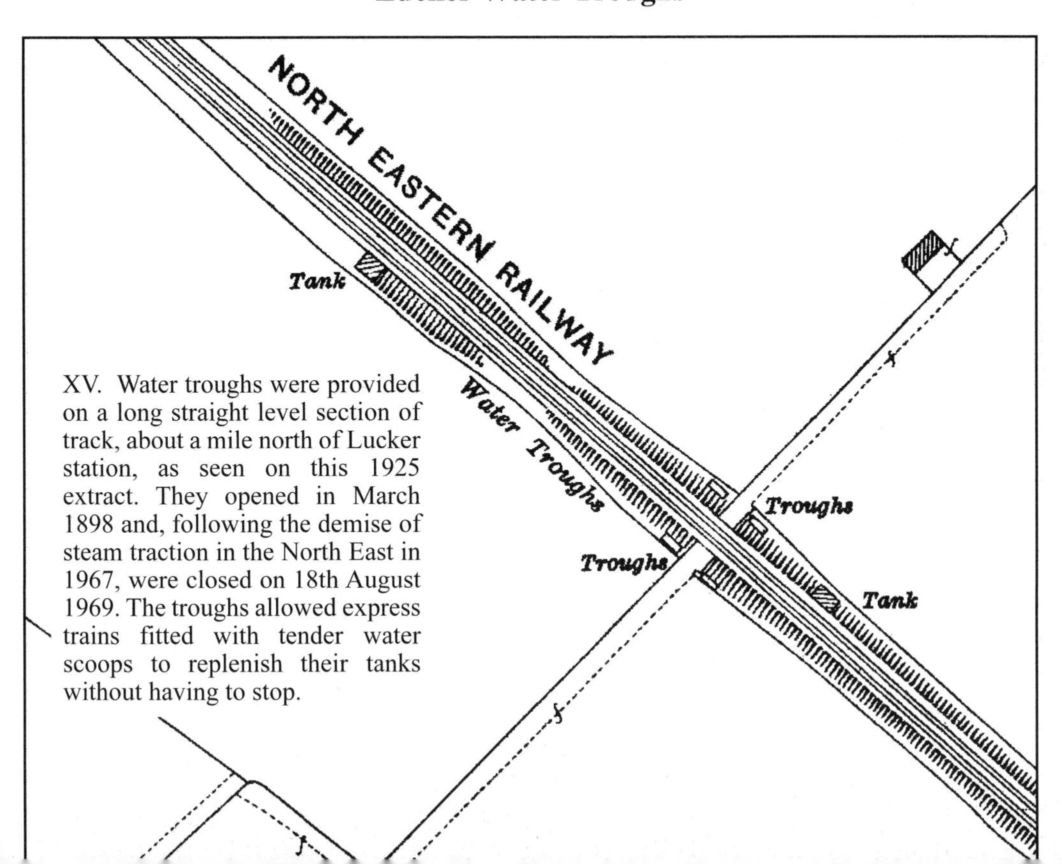

XV. Water troughs were provided on a long straight level section of track, about a mile north of Lucker station, as seen on this 1925 extract. They opened in March 1898 and, following the demise of steam traction in the North East in 1967, were closed on 18th August 1969. The troughs allowed express trains fitted with tender water scoops to replenish their tanks without having to stop.

58. Situated one mile north of Lucker, the troughs were fed by the Newlands Burn. Looking north, we view the instructions to lower the tender scoop. At night, lit only by the oil lamp, it must have been difficult to spot. (J.C.Dean/NERA)

59. This was the water tank for the Up-line trough. In the middle distance is the similar tank for the Down line. This shows the detail of a railway feature long gone from the scene. These troughs were taken out of use on 18th August 1969 and then dismantled. (J.C.Dean/NERA)

60. NER class R (later D20) 4-4-0 no. 1078 is heading a Down express passenger train and picking up water from the troughs. Built in June 1907 the loco was renumbered no. 2383 and then 62383 and withdrawn in May 1957. (K.Taylor/NERA)

61. In August 1955, A4 class 4-6-2 no. 60024 *Kingfisher* on the Down 'Flying Scotsman' was also picking up water. It was not advisable to travel in the coach behind the engine in case the fireman misjudged the level of water in the tender. *Kingfisher* was built in December 1936 and withdrawn in September 1966. (J.W.Armstrong/ARPT)

BELFORD

XVI. The station opened with the line on 29th March 1847. It remained open to goods traffic until 7th June 1968, having lost its passenger services on 29th January 1968. The station building remains in residential use and the former coal staiths are derelict in the former goods yard. This map is dated 1924.

The line branching off to the right goes to Easington (also known as Belford) Quarry. Passing loops were installed by the LNER in 1931 on the mile section between Belford and Crag Mill (see next section). The loops remain in use today. Belford station is closed and Chathill is the limit of the local passenger service from Newcastle. Each train, once empty, travels from Chathill to Belford to cross from Down to Up line and return to Chathill. So far, the authorities have declined to re-open Belford station. Some sidings remain in place for engineering and other purposes.

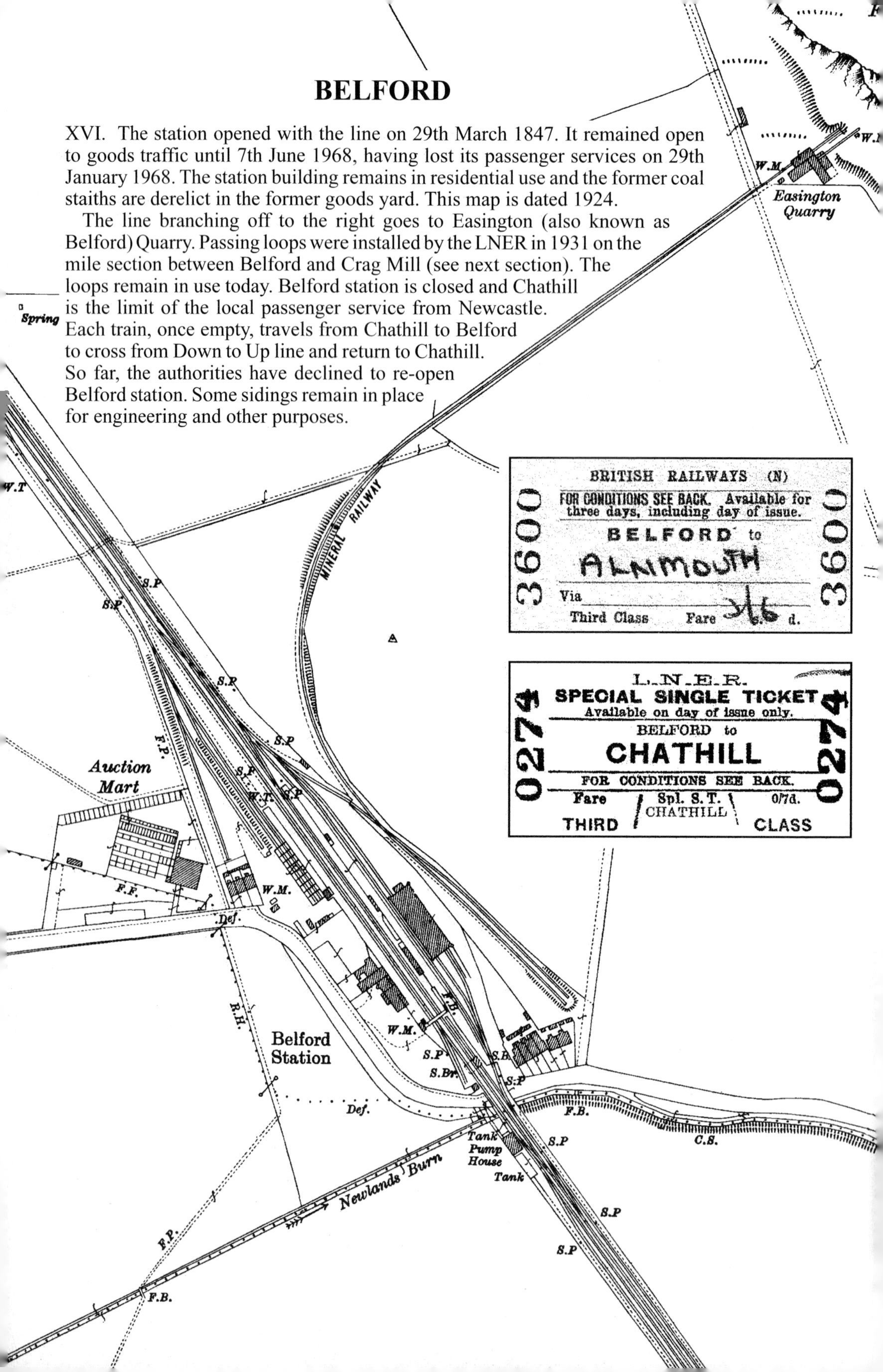

62. This aerial photograph was taken on 1st July 1959 and shows the station, goods shed and coal drops. The elevated NER signal cabin stretched across the tracks. This was the official station for Bamburgh though not the nearest. The prominent station building is now Grade II listed. (E.Colling/D.R.Dunn coll.)

63. The old and new signal boxes were photographed on 24th August 1962. The old was a NER N3 style bridge cabin. It had 52 levers and opened about 1901. It closed on 25th February 1963 when the modern box (similar to the one at Tweedmouth) replaced it. That, in turn, closed on 8th July 1990. (J.M.Fleming)

64. Is this an interloper? Great Western Railway 4-4-0 no. 3440 *City of Truro* is travelling light engine towards Newcastle. Part of the National Collection, the loco spent the war years stored in the Borders. Here it was returning from the Scottish Industries Exhibition held in Glasgow from 3rd to 14th September 1959. (M.Halbert coll.)

65. A pigeon special shows another lost railway scene. Racing pigeons were collected and taken to a station and released for the race from the race station. This pigeon special was in the loop by the goods shed. Now pigeon racers have specially designed articulated lorries (but they retain the wicker baskets!). (ARPT)

66. A type 4 class 40 1-Co-Co-1DE is south of the station with an up passenger train. The station is dwarfed by the grain silos. Coastal Grains Ltd was founded in 1982 and has added four more very large silos in 2015, with plans for another four. It might be feasible to rail connect the site as the sidings exist and are used for storing permanent way units. (G.W.Morrison)

Belford Quarry

67. Another Type 4 1-Co-Co-1DE, this time class 45 no. D63, heads a train loading with ballast on the short branch to Easington quarry. This quarry, later known as Belford quarry, has always been shunted by main line locomotives. The quarry is currently closed, and the branch has been mothballed just in case the quarry re-opens. In this area, over the years, there have been six narrow gauge quarry lines, two near Belford and four near Budle or Bamburgh. All are closed and removed. (M.Halbert coll.)

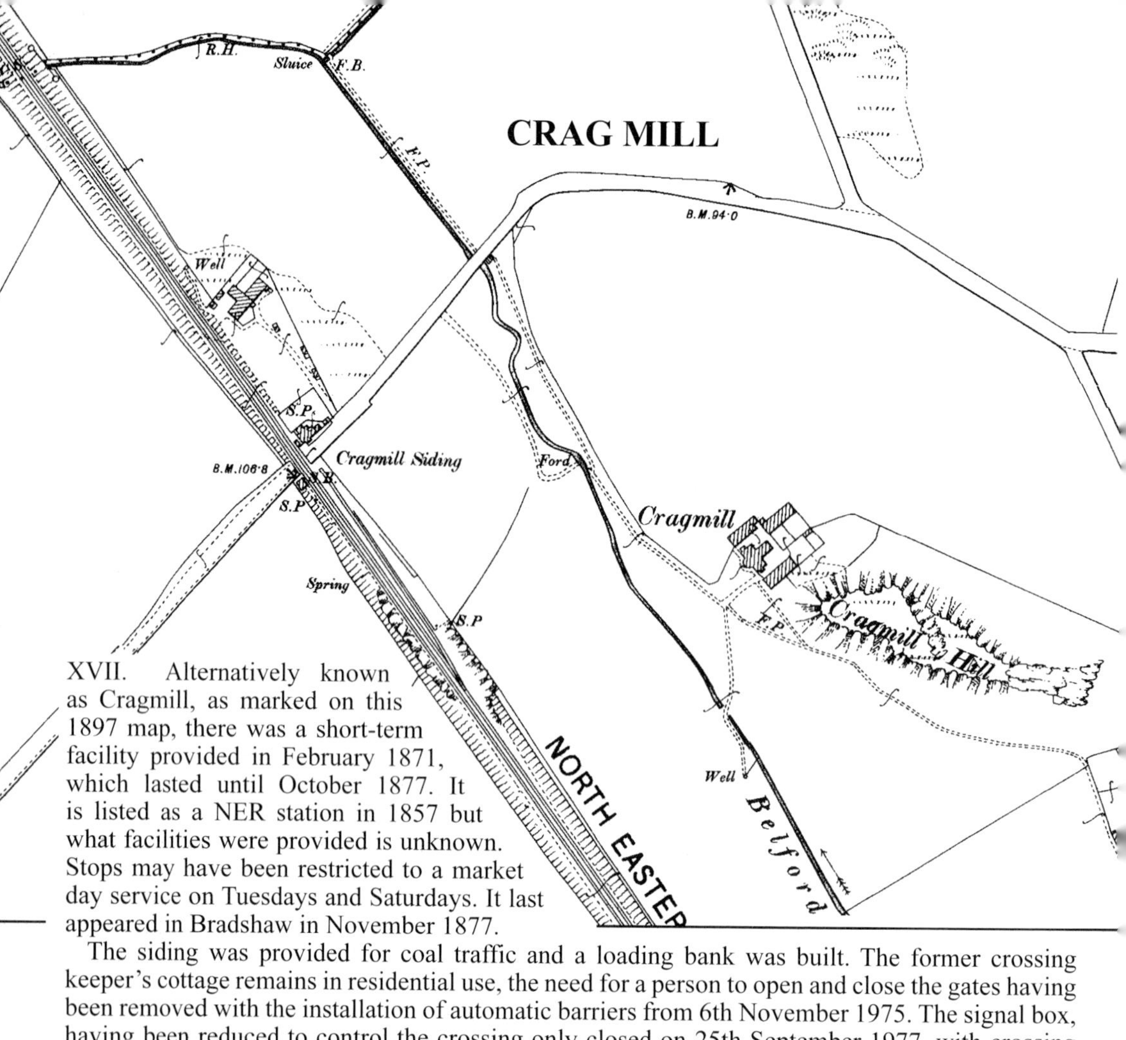

XVII. Alternatively known as Cragmill, as marked on this 1897 map, there was a short-term facility provided in February 1871, which lasted until October 1877. It is listed as a NER station in 1857 but what facilities were provided is unknown. Stops may have been restricted to a market day service on Tuesdays and Saturdays. It last appeared in Bradshaw in November 1877.

The siding was provided for coal traffic and a loading bank was built. The former crossing keeper's cottage remains in residential use, the need for a person to open and close the gates having been removed with the installation of automatic barriers from 6th November 1975. The signal box, having been reduced to control the crossing only closed on 25th September 1977, with crossing control using CCTV passing to Belford.

68. These are the signal box, crossing, gate keeper's hut and crossing keeper's cottage as they were in 1967 looking north. This has been registered as a station, though there has been no evidence of platforms. The cottage is brick-built rather than stone, suggesting later construction in the 1850s. (J.C.Dean/NERA)

69. An Up through freight hauled by V2 class 2-6-2 no. 60806 is approaching the crossing. The class was regularly used on ECML freight, but could also distinguish themselves on passenger trains when required. Built in August 1937, this loco was withdrawn in September 1966. (M.Halbert coll.)

70. The loading bay, which still exists, has a departmental coach parked alongside as class A3 4-6-2 no. 60089 *Felstead* approaches with a class C fitted freight train. Built in August 1928 at Doncaster, this loco survived until October 1963. (M.Halbert coll.)

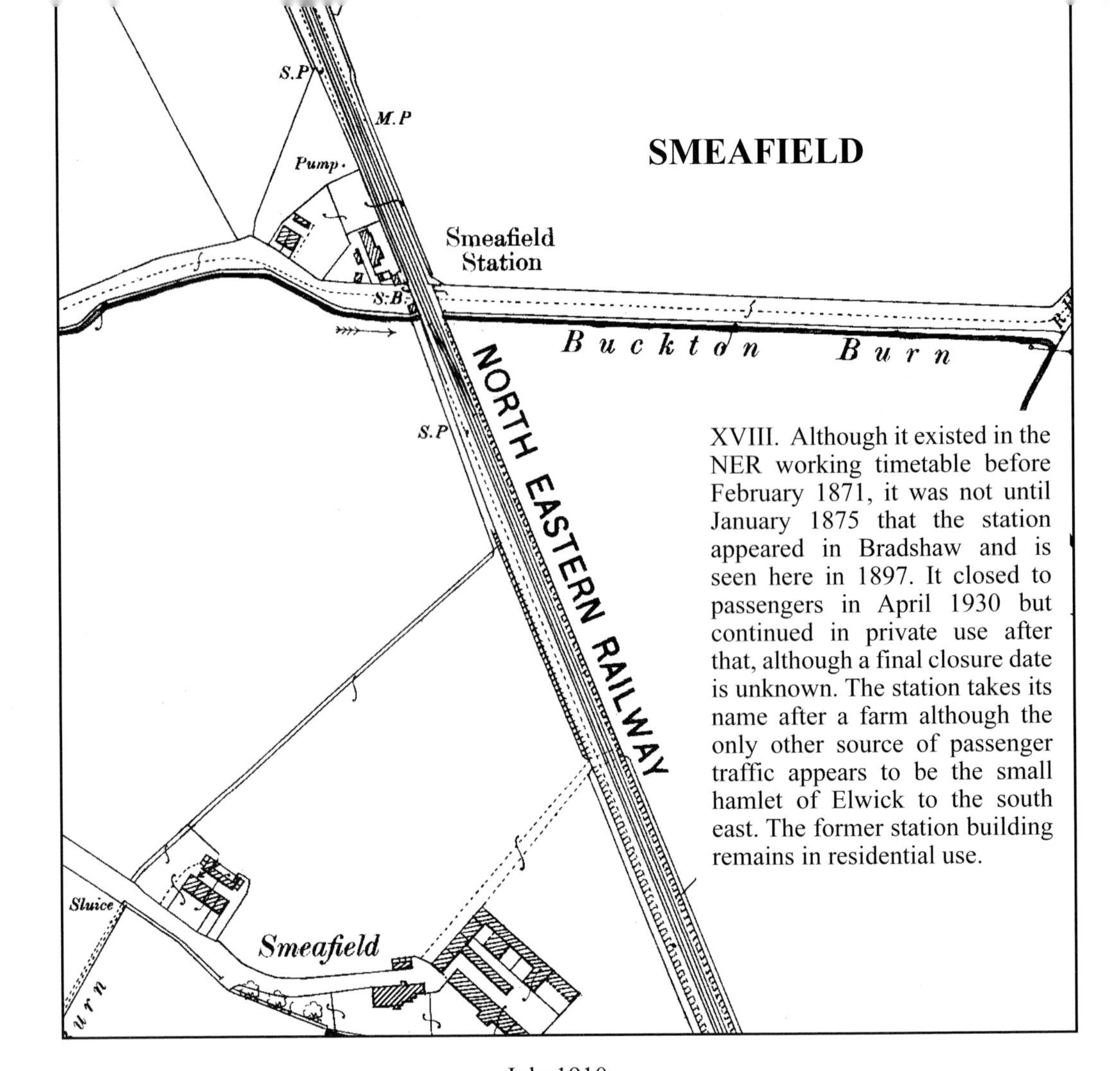

XVIII. Although it existed in the NER working timetable before February 1871, it was not until January 1875 that the station appeared in Bradshaw and is seen here in 1897. It closed to passengers in April 1930 but continued in private use after that, although a final closure date is unknown. The station takes its name after a farm although the only other source of passenger traffic appears to be the small hamlet of Elwick to the south east. The former station building remains in residential use.

July 1910

YORK, NEWCASTLE, BERWICK, and EDINBURGH.—North Eastern.

Miles.	Down. Week Days.	mrn	mrn	mrn	mrn	mrn	mrn	mrn	mrn	mrn	aft	mrn	aft	aft	aft	aft	aft	aft	aft	aft	aft	aft	aft
	684 York ....dep.	1 14	3b35	3b35	3 45	....	....	....	5 55	7 40	....	9 57	....	....	....	....	....	....	....		2 5	....	....
	684 Darlington (B.T) „	2 11	4b41	4b41	4 51	....	....	....	7 52	9 5	....	11 6	....	....	....	....	....	....	....		2 58	....	....
—	New-castle Central dep.	3 8	5 48	6 0	6 20	6 45	7 13	8 10	9 35	1027	....	1212	....	....	1238	1 13	1 30	....	2 27		3 55	....	4 15
½	Manors East	....	5 50	....	....	6 47	....	8 12	....	1029	....		....	....	1240	....	1 32	....	2 29		....	....	4 17
1¾	Heaton	....	5 55	....	....	6 52	7 18	8 17	....	1034	....		....	....	1245	1 19	1 37	....	2 34	Saturdays only.	....	....	4 22
5	Forest Hall	....	m	....	6 30	6 59	....	8 25	....	1041	....		....	....	1252	....	1 44	....	2 41		....	....	4 29
6	Killingworth	....	....	....	....	7 3	....	8 29	....	1045	....	Luncheon Car Express.	....	....	1255	....	1 48	....	2 44		....	....	4 33
7¾	Annitsford	....	....	....	6 37	7 8	....	8 34	....	1050	....		....	....	1 0	....	1 53	....	2 49		....	....	4 38
10	Cramlington	....	....	....	6 42	7 13	....	8 40	....	1056	....		....	....	1 6	....	2 0	....	2 55		....	....	4 43
11½	Plessey	....	....	....	....	7 17	....	8 45	....	11 0	....		....	....	1 10	....	2 5	....	2 59		....	....	4 48
14	Stannington	....	....	....	6 50	7 23	....	8 51	....	11 6	....		....	....	1 16	....	2 11	....	3 5		....	....	4 53
16½	Morpeth 694, 817	....	6 53	c	7 1	7 29	7 40	9 2	9 59	1116	....	1238	....	1 5	1 22	1 45	2 23	....	3 11	3 14	4 19	....	5i19
18½	Pegswood	....		....	....	....	....	9 7	....	1120	....	....	....	1 9	....	1 49	2 27	....	....	3 18	....	....	5 23
20¼	Longhirst	....		....	....	....	....	9 11	....	1124	....	....	....	1 13	....	1 53	2 32	....	....	3 22	....	....	5 27
23¼	Widdrington	....	Via Backworth, see page 694.	....	....	....	....	9 18	....	1131	....	....	....	1 20	....	2 0	2 39	....	....	3 29	....	....	5 34
25½	Chevington 695	....		....	....	....	....	9 24	h	1148	....	....	....	1 26	....	2 5	2 47	....	....	3 35	....	....	5l52
28½	Acklington, for Felton	....		c	7 18	....	....	9 30	....	1154	....	....	....		....	2 12	2 54	....	....	3 41	4 35	....	5 58
31¾	Warkworth	....		....	....	....	8 0	9 37	....	12 0	....	....	....		....	2 19	3 1	....	....	3 48	4 41	....	6 5
34¾	Alnmouth 692 ....arr.	....		6 42	7 29	....	8 6	9 42	1021	12 6	....	1 1	....		....	2 25	3 8	....	....	3 53	4 46	....	6 11
37¾	692 Alnwick ....arr.	....		6 55	7 44	....	8 16	9 57	1044	1218	....	1 22	m		....	2 53	3 20	....	....	4 5	5 2	m	6 25
—	Alnmouth ....dep.	....		6 44	7 40	....	....	9 46	1024	....	1215	1 5	1 18		....		....	3 18	....	....	4 49	5 0	....
37½	Longhoughton	....	....	....	....	....	....	9 53	....	....	1221	....	1 24		....		....	3 24	....	....	....	5 6	....
39½	Little Mill	....	....	....	....	....	....	10 0	....	....	1226	....	1 29	Saturdays only. Arrives Amble 1 41 aft., see page 695.	....		....	3 29	....	....	....	5 11	....
43	Christon Bank	....	....	....	....	....	....	10 7	....	....	1233	....	1 36		....	Saturdays only.	....	3 36	....	....	....	5 18	....
46	Chathill 692	....	....	....	7 56	....	....	1014	....	....	1238	1 23	1 41		....		....	3 41	....	....	5 5	5 23	....
47	Newham	....	....	....	....	....	....	1019	....	....	1243	....	1 46		....		....	3 46	....	....	....	5 28	....
49¼	Lucker	....	....	....	....	....	....	1024	....	....	1248	....	1 51		....		....	3 51	....	....	....	5 33	....
51½	Belford	....	....	c	8 6	....	....	1031	1048	....	1253	1 37	1 56		....		....	3 58	....	....	5 15	5 38	....
55	Smeafield	....	....	....	....	....	....	d	....	....	....	....	d		....		....	....	....	....	....	k	....
58½	Beal	....	....	....	8 17	....	....	11a7	11 1	....	1 4	....	2 7		....		....	4 11	....	....	....	5 49	....
60¾	Goswick	....	....	....	8 22	....	....	1112	....	....	1 8	....	2 11		....		....	4 15	....	....	....	5 53	....
63½	Scremerston	....	....	....	....	....	....	1118	....	....	1 14	....	2 17		....		....	4 21	....	....	....	5 59	....
65¾	Tweedmouth 689	....	....	....	8 33	....	....	1127	....	....	1 23	....	2 25		....		....	4 29	....	....	5 37	6 7	....
67	Berwick 689, 794 arr.	4 36	....	7 23	8 36	....	....	1130	1114	....	1 26	1 58	2 28		....		....	4 32	....	....	5 40	6 10	....
124½	794 Edinburgh (W.) arr.	5 55	....	8 58	10¾g	....	....	....	1245	....	....	3 30	....		....	....	....	....	....	....	....	....	....

a Arrives at 10 43 mrn.
b Except Mondays.
c Stops when required to take up for Edinburgh and beyond.
d Stops on Tuesdays and Saturdays when required.
g Wednesdays only.
h Arrives at 11 36 mrn.
i Arrives at 4 59 aft.
k Stops on Mondays and Saturdays if required.
k Arrives at 8 50 aft.
l Arrives at 5 39 aft.
m Auto-car.
n Stops when required to set down.

71. A1 class 4-6-2 no. 60159 *Auld Reekie* was on the 11.00 Kings Cross to Edinburgh passing through the station. The main station buildings were on the Down side. This was the nearest station to Ross Links, a remote area on the coast that had a complex target railway on a military range. (H.B.Priestley/R.Humm coll.)

72. This is a general view of the station in 1967. It started life as Elwick Gate suggesting it was a crossing keeper's cottage, but it might have been a private station until 1875 when it first appeared in the timetables. It did have two platforms facing each other with the buildings on the Down line and no buildings at all on the Up platform. It also had no goods facilities. (J.C.Dean/NERA)

73. The platforms were last used in 1958. The station buildings are fenced off as a private house. The station closed at the end of 1929 but may have been used 'unofficially' for some time after that. The 1877 signal box had a ten-lever frame. It was closed on 9th December 1973 and demolished shortly after. (J.W.Armstrong/ARPT)

74. By 1967, the platforms had gone but the platform milepost was still there. Here is another word about the Ross Links target railway. The Links had been a firing range since 1899, but in 1942 a 2ft 6in gauge railway was laid. Self-propelled target trolleys were built by Wickham. In use, the trolleys carried a large silhouette of a tank. The aim was to hit the target not the trolley, which was screened by an embankment. The railway was used until 1958 when it was transferred to Redesdale. Some trolleys were still there in 2018. (J.C.Dean/NERA)

BEAL

XIX. Beal was the nearest station to the Holy Island of Lindisfarne, often referred to as simply Holy Island. The station opened on 29th March 1847 and would have carried many seeking solace there. This 1897 map shows the station, which opened on 29th March 1847. It closed to goods traffic on 26th April 1965 and to passengers on 29th January 1968. The station was demolished in 1979. Lindisfarne is connected to the mainland by a road that is submerged at high tide and can be used only at certain times of the day.

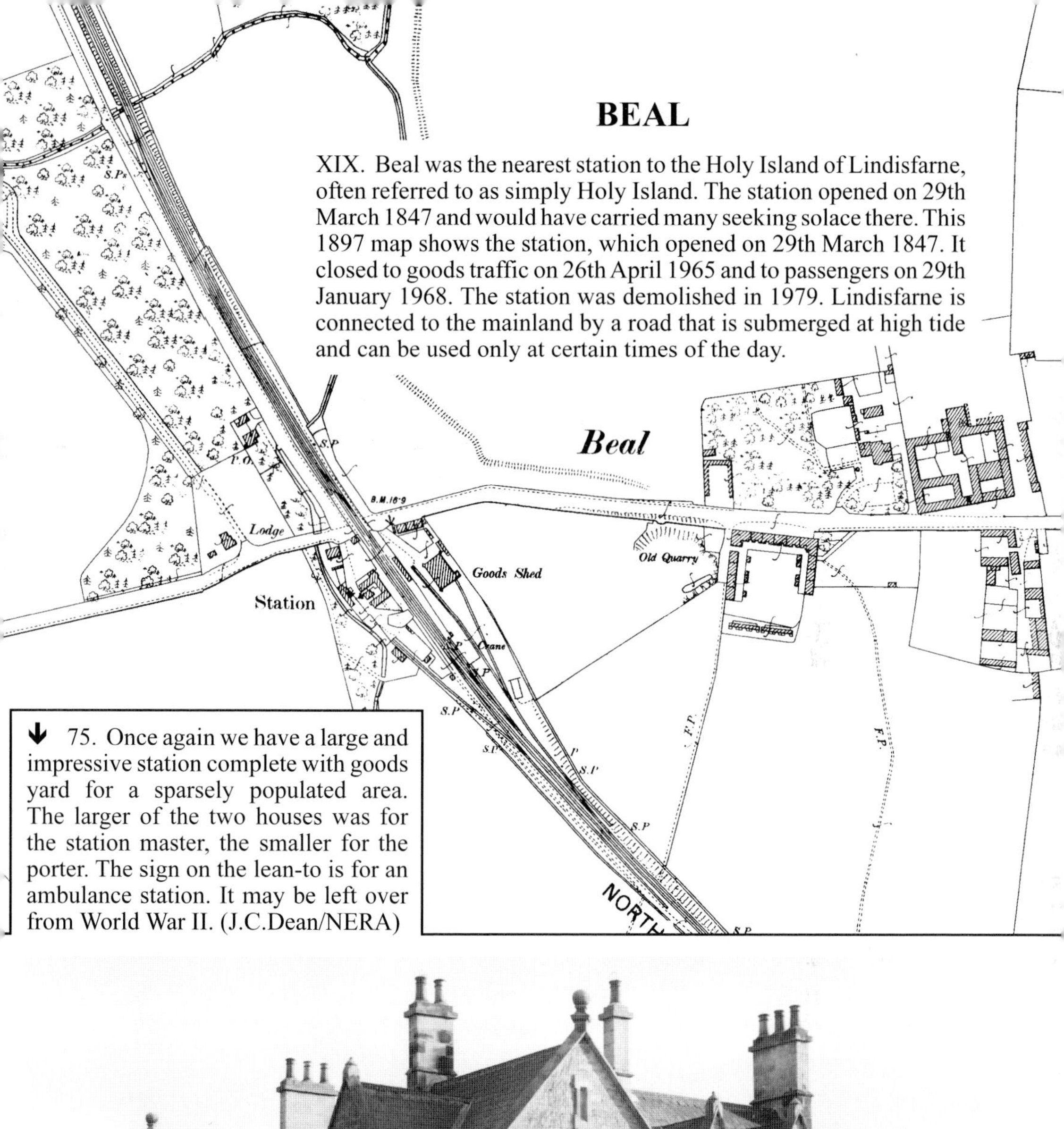

↓ 75. Once again we have a large and impressive station complete with goods yard for a sparsely populated area. The larger of the two houses was for the station master, the smaller for the porter. The sign on the lean-to is for an ambulance station. It may be left over from World War II. (J.C.Dean/NERA)

76. A general view of the signal box and station shows that passengers crossed the line on the left, for no footbridge was provided. The signal box was from the 1870s. A new 31-lever frame was installed in 1958 and it was closed on 18th April 1982. (J.C.Dean/NERA)

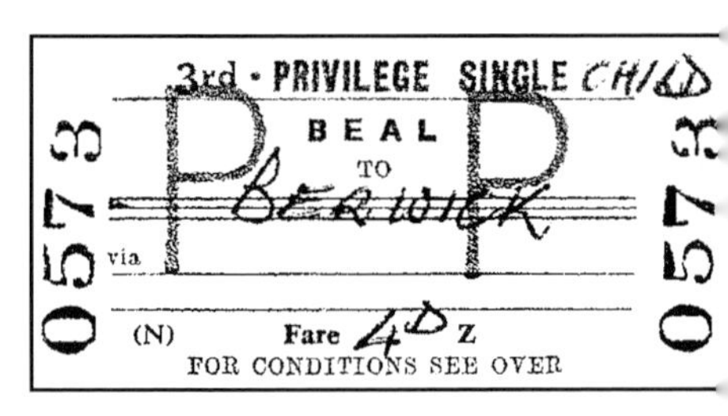

77. At the station we look to the south as class B16 4-6-0 no. 61472 is coming through light engine. The B16 class (NER class S3) was built for fast goods trains but was often seen on passenger workings, especially summer excursions. No. 61472 was built in December 1919 and lasted until September 1961. (J.W.Armstrong/ARPT)

78. A Derby-built lightweight DMU was heading south on 14th August 1960. These were the first generation of DMUs built for British Railways in 1954. Numbered in the 79xxx series, most were withdrawn by the end of the 1960s. (N.E.Stead/Transport Library)

79. In a garden that was part of the goods yard and south east of the level crossing, is the privately preserved 0-4-0ST Peckett 1611 of 1923. The date was 13th August 2014. The loco worked at Courtaulds Coventry, then at Albright & Wilson, and came to this site via the Swanage Railway. (M.T.Snowball)

HOLY ISLAND

Three separate narrow gauge tram lines were built at various times from 1846 on Lindisfarne to transport limestone to a jetty for onward transport by sea. All appear to have been worked by horse power. These have long since closed with the limestone industry coming to an end in the mid-1880s. Kilns were built to burn the lime, and coal to heat them would have been brought in by sea and conveyed by the wagon way to the kilns. Some of the old formations can be followed by walkers on the island.

80. This shows the eastern trackbed of the horse-drawn railway that in one way and another circumnavigated the island. The gauge was probably 2ft. A steam locomotive was tried but it derailed too often. The lime kilns are the Castle Point kilns and the ship loading point was to the right and behind the castle. The kilns were top fed and bottom emptied. Ships took the lime products to Berwick, Newcastle and London. (Geograph 4686912 reproduced under creative common licence)

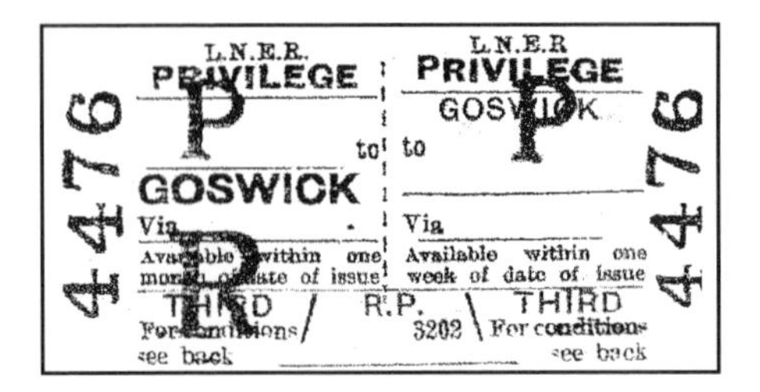

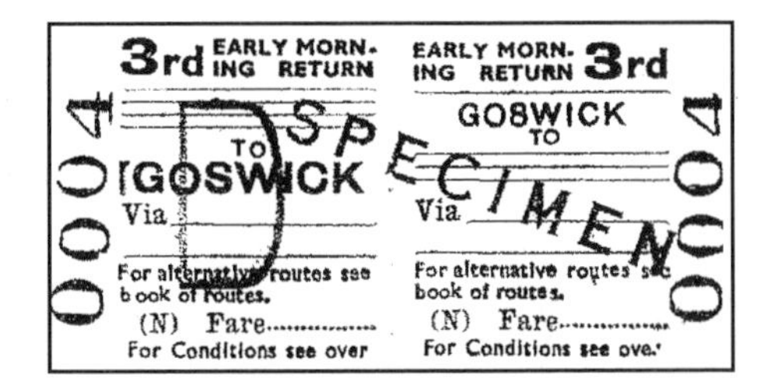

GOSWICK

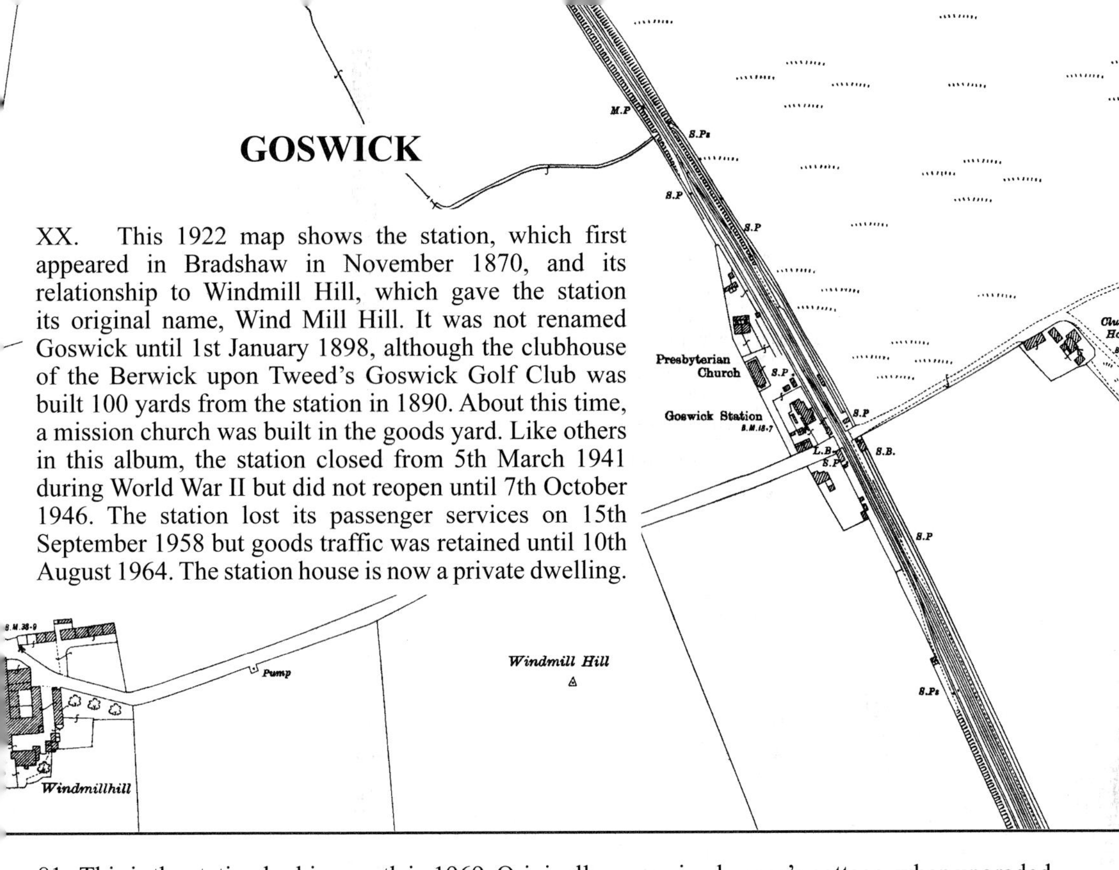

XX. This 1922 map shows the station, which first appeared in Bradshaw in November 1870, and its relationship to Windmill Hill, which gave the station its original name, Wind Mill Hill. It was not renamed Goswick until 1st January 1898, although the clubhouse of the Berwick upon Tweed's Goswick Golf Club was built 100 yards from the station in 1890. About this time, a mission church was built in the goods yard. Like others in this album, the station closed from 5th March 1941 during World War II but did not reopen until 7th October 1946. The station lost its passenger services on 15th September 1958 but goods traffic was retained until 10th August 1964. The station house is now a private dwelling.

81. This is the station looking north in 1969. Originally a crossing keeper's cottage, when upgraded to a station, it had platforms staggered either side of the crossing. There was one goods siding. The 1877 signal box was on the Down side but in 1901 a new box was built on the Up side; it closed on 28th March 1982. (J.C.Dean/NERA)

82. We are looking south this time. In 1901 the NER improved capacity on the Main Line by building long loops to accommodate slower trains, mainly freight, and to let fast passenger trains through. The NER called them 'Independents'; they were early versions of 'dynamic loops'. An Up Independent between Goswick and Beal was built in 1901 and the Down Independent was added in 1918. Both were removed in August 1966. (J.C.Dean/NERA)

83. Goswick was the site of two serious accidents. The first was on 28th August 1907, when a freight train over-ran signals and derailed. The locomotive was NER class S (LNER B13) 4-6-0 no. 2005 and it ended upside down in a ditch. Two people were killed and another seriously injured. Here, the crowds watch as the locomotive is lifted. (ARPT)

84. On 26th October 1947 the Up 'Flying Scotsman' failed to slow for a diversion to the loop and derailed. 28 people were killed and 65 injured from the 420 people on the train. The locomotive was A3 class 4-6-2 no. 66 *Merry Hampton*. The train jack-knifed and the locomotive was almost buried. *Merry Hampton* was the locomotive derailed by miners at Cramlington in 1926.
(M.Halbert coll.)

July 1899 ➔

LEEDS, NORMANTON, YORK, DARLINGTON, DURHAM, SHIELDS, SUNDERLAND, NEWCASTLE, MORPETH, & BERWICK.—N.E.

Down. — **Week Days**—*Continued on page 480.*

Down.
St. Pancras Station, London 418 ....dep.
" (Euston) 310 "
459 Birmnghm (NewSt) "
419 Derby (StationSt.) "
419 Sheffield (Sta. Rd) "
574 L'pool (Exchange) "
384 " (Lime St.) "
546 Manchester (Vic.) "
394 " (Ex.) via Leeds "
Leeds New Sta. dep.
Leeds Marsh Lane "
Cross Gates
Garforth
Micklefield
Normanton ......dep.
Castleford
Burton Salmon
Milford 492 ......arr.
Hull (v. Milford) 494 d
Milford ......dep.
Sherburn
Harrogate 505 ..dep.
Church Fenton 505
Ulleskelf
Bolton Percy
Copmanthorpe
York 498, 505, 493 ar
418 London (St. Pan.) dep.
459 Birmnghm (NewSt) "
419 Derby (Sta. St.) "
477 Sheffield (Sta. Rd) "
493 Hull (Paragon) 494 "
262 London (King's Crs.) "
Doncaster 263 "
York ......dep.
Beningbrough
Tollerton
Alne 504
Raskelf 492
Pilmoor 505
Sessay
384 L'pool (Lime St.) dep.
394 Manchester (Ex.) "
500 Leeds (New Sta.) "
Thirsk 502
Otterington ......(501
Northallerton 500, 511
Stockton 500 ....arr.
500 West Hartlepool "
Middlesbro' 508 "
Danby Wiske
Cowton
Dalton 489
Croft Spa
Darlington (Bank Top) 508, 509 arr.
Darlington dep.
Aycliffe
Bradbury
Ferryhill 503, 507, 477
Ferryhill
Shincliffe
Sherburn Colliery
Leamside 490
Durham 490, 504 dep.
Durham arr.
Sunderland 490 arr.
Fencehouses
Penshaw 490
Washington
Usworth
Pelaw 511
South Shields ....arr.
Sunderland ...... "
Felling
Gateshead (East)
Ferryhill ......dep.
Croxdale
Durham 504, 490
Plawsworth
Chester-le-Street
Birtley 493
Lamesley
Low Fell
Bensham
Gateshead (West)
Newcastle 488, 510 arr. to 513, 489, 602
Newcastle ......dep.
Heaton
Forest Hall
Killingworth
Annitsford
Cramlington
Plessey
Stannington
Morpeth 510, 602
Longhirst
Widdrington
Chevington 477
Acklington (for Felton)
Warkworth
Alnmouth ¶
¶ Alnwick 511 dep.
¶ Alnwick arr.
Longhoughton
Little Mill
Christon Bank
Chathill 489
Newham
Lucker
Belford
Beal
Goswick
Scremerston
Tweedmouth 489
Berwick 598, 489 ....arr.
598 Edinbro' (Wav.) arr.
Glasgow * 610 "
Dundee † 604 "
Aberdeen † 604 "
Perth † 603 "

SOUTH OF SCREMERSTON

Scremerston Lime Works

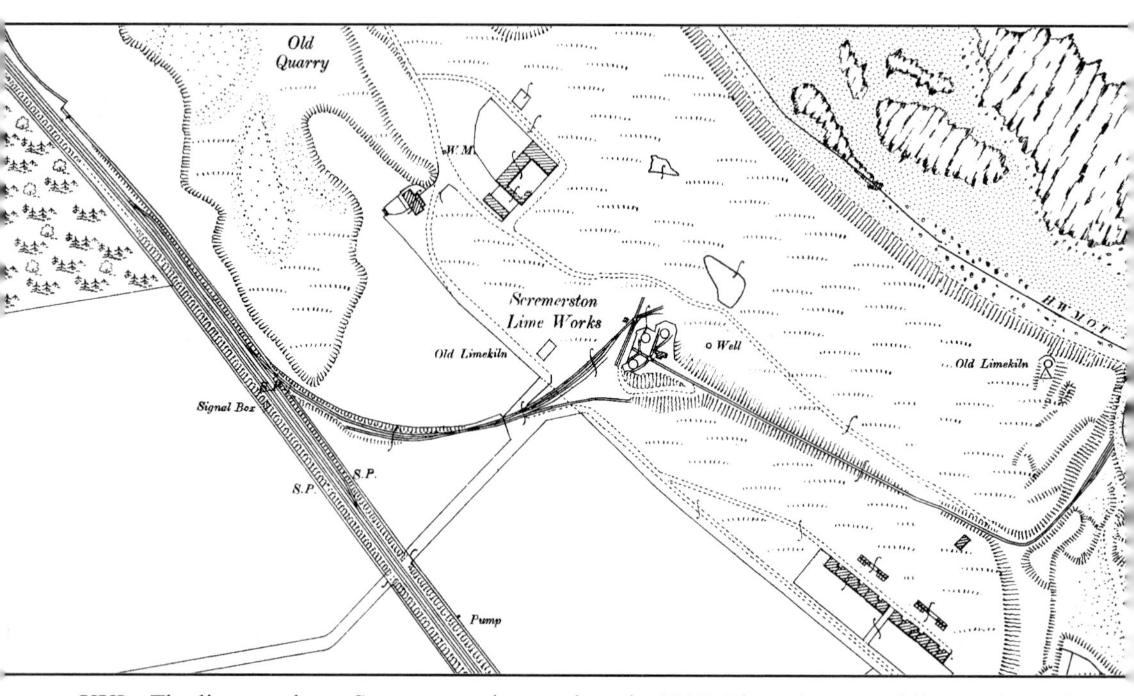

XXI. The lime works at Scremerston is seen here in 1897. The existence of limeworks in the area predates the railway. The first, known as Saltpan How, was in operation before 1824 and was not connected to the Newcastle & Berwick Railway. Although it had an internal narrow-gauge tramway of unknown gauge, it relied on horses and carts to take the limestone to Scremerston station for onward transit via the station's lime depot. It was closed by the 1880s and the former quarry was subsequently filled in over many years with domestic waste from the Berwick area.

A second lime works opened in the 1860s on the site seen above and was connected to the Main Line by a north-facing junction. Again, there was an internal narrow gauge horse-drawn network, although a stationary engine was used to haul wagons up an incline to take them towards the kilns, returning to horse power for the final stage of the journey. After being crushed, the limestone was loaded into standard gauge wagons for onward movement to the Main Line. Coal was brought in and limestone taken out was hauled by a Tweedmouth-allocated locomotive. The short branch into the works was controlled by Scremerston Lime Works signal box.

Quarrying of limestone ceased in 1900 and, over time, the quarry disappeared under Berwick's domestic waste. The kilns survived until the early 1980s when they were demolished, although the houses for the quarry workers, seen towards the bottom of the map, had been demolished prior to the outbreak of World War II. With the quarries infilled and returned to agricultural use, today there are few clues to their existence.

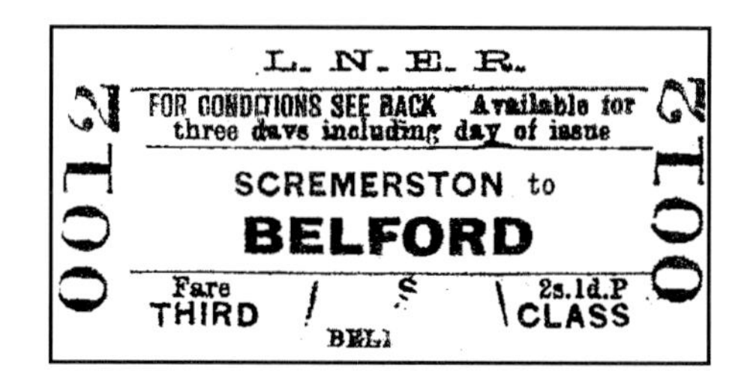
L. N. E. R.
FOR CONDITIONS SEE BACK Available for three days including day of issue
SCREMERSTON to
BELFORD
Fare 2s.1d.P
THIRD CLASS
0012
0012

SCREMERSTON

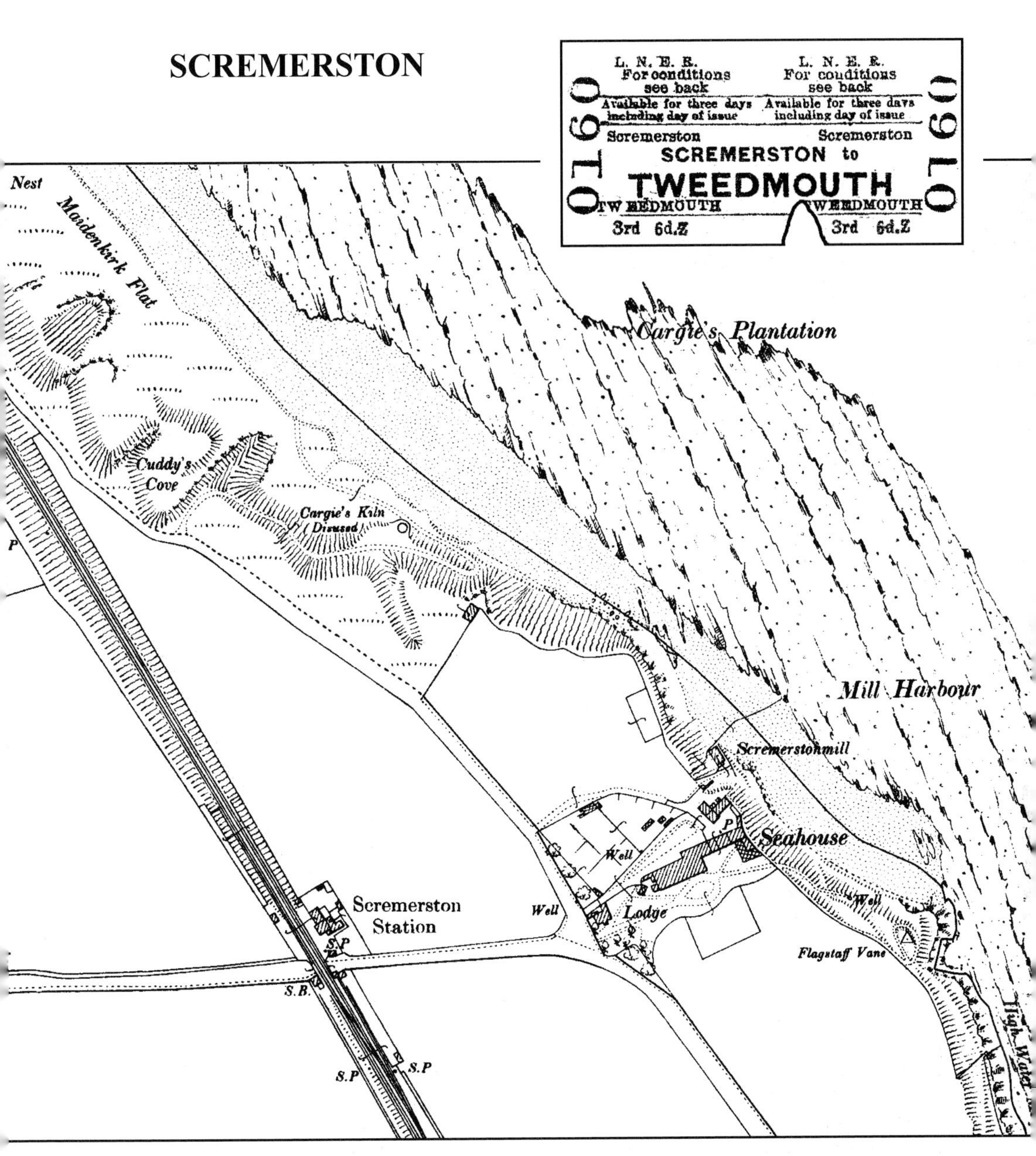

XXII. The station, seen here in 1897, opened on 29th March 1847 and, like many others in this album, it closed from 5th May 1941 until 7th October 1946. One Down (northbound) train stopped to set down newspapers during the temporary wartime closure, although on Saturdays this was an Up (southbound) working. Final closure to passenger traffic occurred on 9th July 1951, the goods yard closing the previous day. The Working Timetable for 1953 shows a set down on Fridays only for railway staff being provided on a northbound train solely, there being no arrangements for Up trains.

85. In 1910 the station and signal box were in the countryside. For the N&B this is a style unlike its other stations, more cottage and less Gothic. The rural scene continued over the years. Even for a wayside station, this must have been uneconomical from the beginning. (ARPT)

86. This is the station facing north with the signal box. The signal box was built in October 1877, was demoted to a gate box on 10th April 1960 and closed on 15th March 1981. The 12-lever frame was increased to 20 in 1907. (J.C.Dean/NERA)

87. An Up semi-fast train passes the signal box on 6th June 1960, hauled by class A2/3 4-6-2 no. 60516 *Hycilla*. Built in November 1946, it was withdrawn in November 1962. A Thompson design, the cylinders were placed too far back to be aesthetically pleasing. (H.B.Priestley/R.Humm coll.)

88. Brush Type 4 Co-CoDE no. D1634 was going north though the station on a fitted van train. Built in 1962, the locomotive was renumbered for TOPS as Class 47 no. 47052 and scrapped in May 1997 (J.C.Dean/NERA)

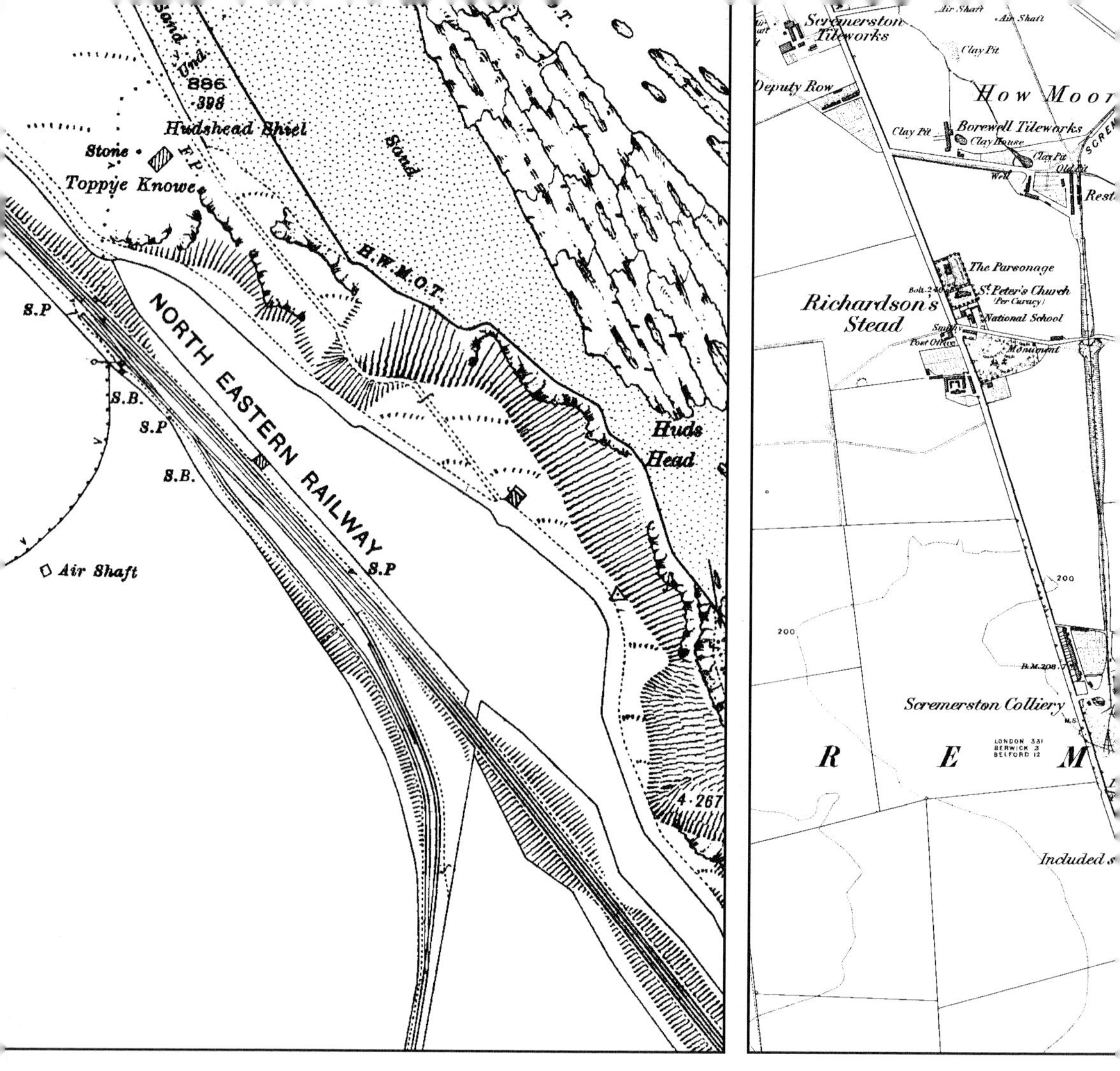

NORTH OF SCREMERSTON

Scremerston Colliery Junction

↑ XXIII. This 1924 map shows the connection with the Main Line for the mineral line, which carried coal out from Scremerston Colliery. Prior to the opening of the Main Line, a waggonway connected the Old Scremerston colliery to an 1810 plateway that led from Huds Head quarry to Carr Rock Jetty on the Tweed.

The waggonway utilised horse-power to haul the trucks to an incline, where a steam-operated winding engine lowered the wagons down the incline. Having reached the lower level at Spittal, horses once again took over to take the wagons to the jetty. The plateway was changed to a railway around the late 1820s. The second Scremerston colliery (Resurrection Pit) was sunk in 1824. With the arrival of the Newcastle & Berwick Railway in the late 1840s, the old formation down to the pier was abandoned and, instead, the line connected with the main line through exchange sidings. The third Scremerston colliery (Greenwich Pit) was further south. Sunk in the 1870s, it lasted until 1944. This junction with the N&B was also known as the Blackhill branch after the name of the major coal seam adding to name confusions in the area.

Another waggonway crossed under the Main Line linking Unthank Colliery with Tweedmouth. The colliery lay some 3½ miles south-west of Berwick and had opened sometime in the 1770s. The waggonway was constructed in 1826, but closed and was removed shortly after the tunnels under the main line had been constructed. Coal mining at Unthank ceased in 1905.

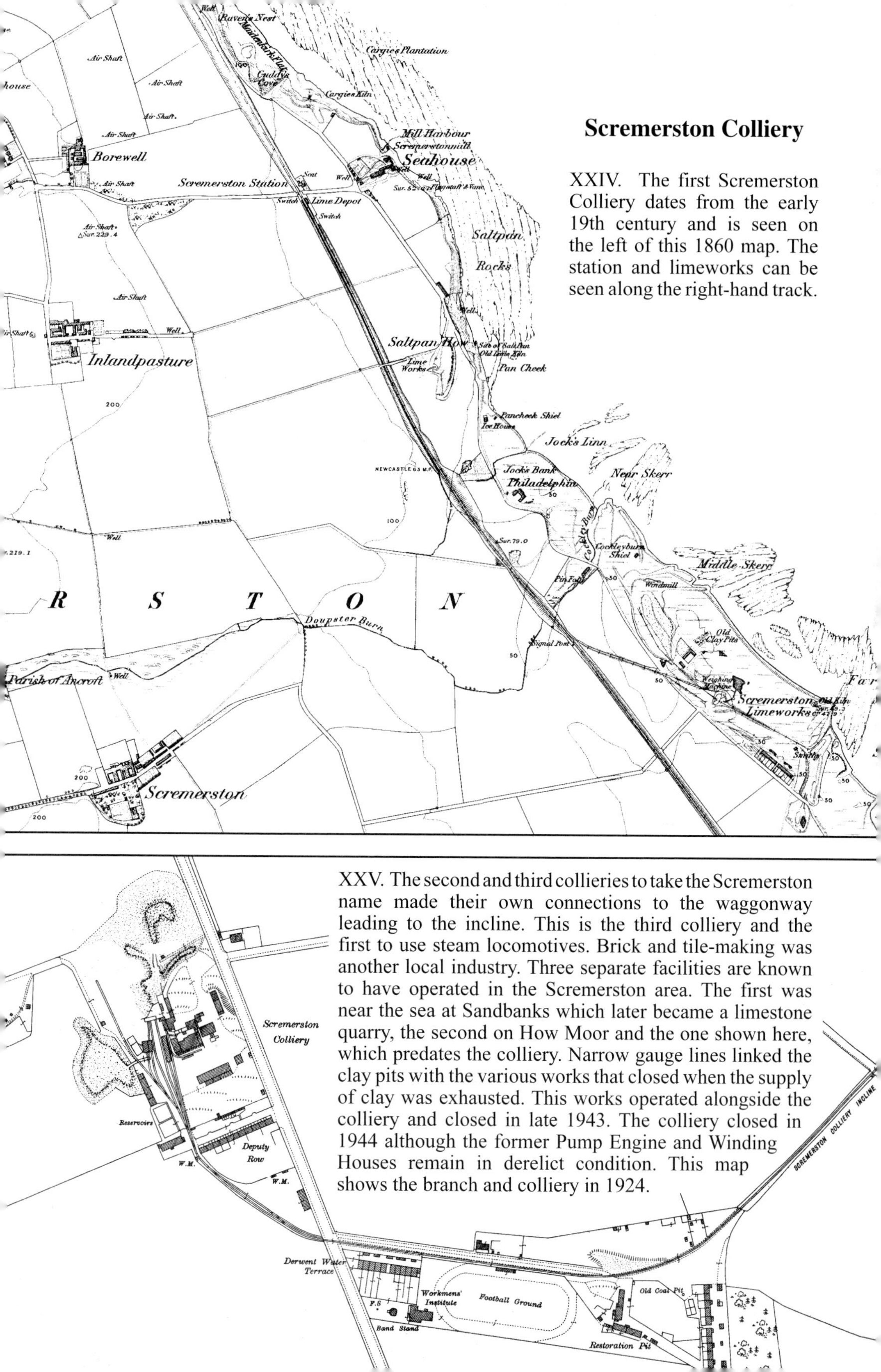

Scremerston Colliery

XXIV. The first Scremerston Colliery dates from the early 19th century and is seen on the left of this 1860 map. The station and limeworks can be seen along the right-hand track.

XXV. The second and third collieries to take the Scremerston name made their own connections to the waggonway leading to the incline. This is the third colliery and the first to use steam locomotives. Brick and tile-making was another local industry. Three separate facilities are known to have operated in the Scremerston area. The first was near the sea at Sandbanks which later became a limestone quarry, the second on How Moor and the one shown here, which predates the colliery. Narrow gauge lines linked the clay pits with the various works that closed when the supply of clay was exhausted. This works operated alongside the colliery and closed in late 1943. The colliery closed in 1944 although the former Pump Engine and Winding Houses remain in derelict condition. This map shows the branch and colliery in 1924.

89. This was the third colliery that was rail connected and called by this name. 0-4-0ST Robert Stephenson's no. 2841 of 1896 was here from 1935 until 1944 when the pit closed. It replaced two earlier locomotives, a Barclay and a Manning Wardle. (R.Jermy coll.)

90. The exchange sidings from the colliery waggonway were situated here. Even in 1967 the trackbed, including the incline, was visible and can still be seen today. The original waggonway passed under the N&BR before the interchange sidings were built. This photograph was labelled 'Blackhill colliery branch'. (J.C.Dean/NERA)

SOUTH OF TWEEDMOUTH

Spittal

XXVI. The East Coast Main Line runs high above the promenade at the seaside village of Spittal, a venue well-known to railway photographers as the hills to the west allow views of trains running along the coast, with Berwick-upon-Tweed providing a backdrop. It is seen here in 1924. Its name is derived from the leper hospital dedicated to St. Bartholomew and recorded in 1234. No station was ever provided here.

The need to move both stone and coal to the coast for onward shipment resulted in several short waggonways being developed early in the 19th century. One was the horse-drawn 'Spittal Railway' built in 1810 to carry stone from the quarry at Huds Head south of Spittal, through the village to construct the pier at Carr Rock (near to the current Tweed Dock). After a period of disuse, the line reopened and was rebuilt from a plateway to a railway and was used until the 1850s.

GNER

← 91. B16 class 4-6-0 no. 61458 is coming down from Scremerston with a mineral train on 1st June 1957. The NER class S3 was the Raven designed culmination of the NER 4-6-0. No. 61458 was built at Darlington in October 1923 and was withdrawn in November 1959. The village of Spittal is below the railway on the left. (N.E.Stead coll./Transport Library)

↙ *(middle)* 92. The speed, quietness and the dark blue livery of the GNER Inter City 225 trains led to their nickname 'Stealth Bombers'. In the early 1990s, class 91 Bo-BoWE 91132 *City of Durham* was coming down past Spittal village. In the distance is Highfields Caravan Park to the north of Berwick. (ARPT)

↙ *(bottom)* 93. This is a painting of the original plateway from Huds Head to Carr Rock in 1822. It was sometimes known as the Spittal Railway. ('A Century of Permanent Way' by F.Bland et al, Berwick Museum/R.Jermy)

Spittal Miniature Railway

Spittal boasts one of the finest beaches in Northumberland, which made it a popular day destination for Sunday School and other outings right up until the mid-1960s. The growth in miniature railways post-war resulted in a scheme for Spittal promenade being developed by a local businessman from Tweedmouth. John Harrison had operated the refreshment rooms at Berwick station and also an ice cream and sweet stall on Spittal promenade. Having acquired a locomotive, coaches and track he set about building a 12in gauge line on derelict land at the sound end of Spittal promenade in 1966. Although track was laid and it is believed that the line did operate briefly, visitors stayed away as it was one of the worst summers on record and visitors were affected by the death of three boys from Leitholm who were on a Sunday School outing and were dragged out to sea following a surge in the tide that had been calm just seconds before. Two other boys were fortunately rescued. The tragedy, not surprisingly, resulted in many similar groups abandoning their visits and, as a result, at the end of the season the short-lived line was lifted and removed to the Olicana Miniature Railway, Ilkley, West Yorkshire.

The locomotive is still in operation and has had a long and interesting history. It was built as a 4-4-2 in 1935 by George Flooks. an engineer in Watford. and named Prince Edward. *He had built the first miniature railway at Bricket Wood between Watford and St. Albans, which opened as a 10¼in line and was converted by Flooks to 12in gauge in 1905 to give greater stability. In 1945 the locomotive was purchased for the line at Ruislip Lido in London, one of the few 12in gauge lines to operate. It was out of use at Ruislip in 1959 before arriving at its next known use at Spittal, before it moved to Ilkley at the end of the 1966 season to the Olicana Park where a new railway was constructed. The line was re-gauged to 10¼in in time for the 1974 season, with the locomotive transferring to the 12¼in gauge Littlehampton Miniature Railway. Due to the ¼in difference in track gauge it was prone to derailment and put into store. Arthur Maxfield, the then owner of the Littlehampton line, secured a concession to operate a miniature railway at Butlin's holiday camp at nearby Bognor Regis. The line at Bognor Regis opened in 1987 and closed in 1992. In 1992 it was purchased for use on a private line in Surrey.*

The southern end of the sea front at Spittal seen here in October 2018. (D.A.Lovett)

Tweedmouth Engine Shed

94. A D20 class (NER class R) 4-4-0 was on shed in 1936. Its number is not clear. Nos. 2027 and 2028 were shedded here in 1937, and 2022 and 2029 in 1938. Otherwise it is a good general view of the shed. (Photomatic/R.Humm coll.)

XXVII. The extensive facilities provided at Tweedmouth can be seen on this 1924 map. The first shed was constructed after 1st July 1847 following the opening of the line from Newcastle, by the Newcastle & Berwick Railway. The modest facilities were improved in 1877 by the building of a new 20-road roundhouse alongside the existing three-road straight engine shed. Part of the goods yard was acquired in 1907 and became the repair shop.

Another major development occurred a year after the Grouping in 1924 when all locomotives used in the Berwick area, belonging to the former North British and North Eastern companies, were concentrated on one depot with Tweedmouth taking over the staff and 21 locomotives from the former North British roundhouse just north of Berwick station. This enabled the latter to be demolished to allow for the rebuilding of Berwick station, which was completed in 1927.

Main Line expresses were the domain of either Newcastle (Gateshead or Heaton) or Edinburgh (Haymarket or St. Margaret's) depots. Tweedmouth was, however, responsible for local branch line working and for Main Line goods traffic in and out of Berwick marshalling yard. It also had a small allocation of locomotives suitable for taking over main line express trains should a failure occur.

Berwick marshalling yard closed early in 1939 and this greatly reduced the allocation of freight locomotives required as locomotives were provided by other depots just as the express trains did, although crews continued to be changed at Tweedmouth. The shed was also responsible for branch line passenger trains over both routes to St. Boswells (either via Duns or Kelso), the Coldstream to Alnmouth route via Alnwick, the Eyemouth branch and for some local stopping trains on the East Coast Main Line, between Edinburgh and Berwick and Berwick and Newcastle.

In BR days the shed was given the shed code 52D. It closed on 19th June 1966. The straight shed was demolished in April 1968, whilst the roundhouse was sold for industrial use. It suffered major fire damage on 14th January 2010 and was demolished in August 2020.

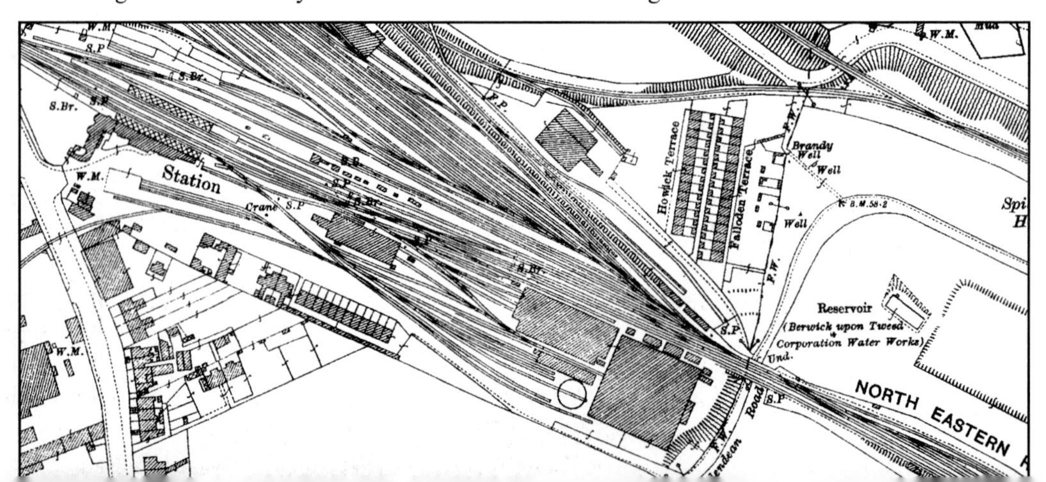

95. There was a side entrance to the roundhouse and 2-6-0 no. 77004 is in the arch. By the time this small class of Standard locomotives had been built the traffic they were built for had been mainly lost. No. 77004 was built in March 1954, came to Tweedmouth in June 1964, went to Stourton in June 1966 and was withdrawn in December of that year. No. 77004 was fitted with a small snowplough. A larger plough is seen to the right. (J.C.Dean/NERA)

96. The interior of the roundhouse in 1961 was home to four class J39 0-6-0 locos, all too grimy to identify. In 1961, Tweedmouth and Alnmouth were allocated nos 64869, 64897 and 64917. All the J39 class had been withdrawn by the end of 1962. The wagon with the stripes is a shock absorber wagon for fragile loads. (Colour-Rail.com)

97. Here is a locomotive from across the Border being turned to return in July 1961. NBR class B (later J37) 0-6-0 no. 64624 was built by the North British Locomotive Co. in January 1921 and was withdrawn in January 1966. The smart appearance, in contrast to those in picture 96, is because it has worked the 'Borders' railtour with 4-4-0 no. 256. (G.Parry/Colour-Rail.com)

98. Class K3 2-6-0 no. 61952 was a local engine allocated to Tweedmouth and on shed on 9th July 1961 with a more exotic visitor. Class D34 (NBR class K) 4-4-0 no. 62469 *Glen Douglas* had been refurbished in NBR livery and given its original number 256 in 1959 and worked special trains and excursions. On this day it had worked the RCTS 'Borders' railtour from Hawick to Greenlaw, St. Boswells, Jedburgh, Kelso and Tweedmouth. At Tweedmouth, no. 256 and no. 64624 were replaced by class A1 4-6-3 no. 60143 *Sir Walter Scott*. It was given to Glasgow Corporation in 1962 and is now in the new Museum of Transport at Glasgow Riverside. (G.W.Morrison)

TWEEDMOUTH

99. Class D17/1 4-4-0 no. 1621 was at the Down platform in 1928. The short train was probably for the Kelso branch. All trains to and from the branch and Berwick used the Down platform, which required reversals as the only lockable points were south of the station. (LGRP/R.Humm coll.)

100. This was the exterior of the station on 11th March 1967. The station buildings were on the Down side. It was a large station as it was effectively the terminus until the Royal Border Bridge was built. The NBR had built their station in the middle of Berwick Castle and George Hudson was not to be outdone even temporarily. The station had a train shed of two spans across the lines, which was removed in 1906. There was also a siding that ran through the station forecourt into the Tweed Saw Mill. (J.C.Dean/NERA)

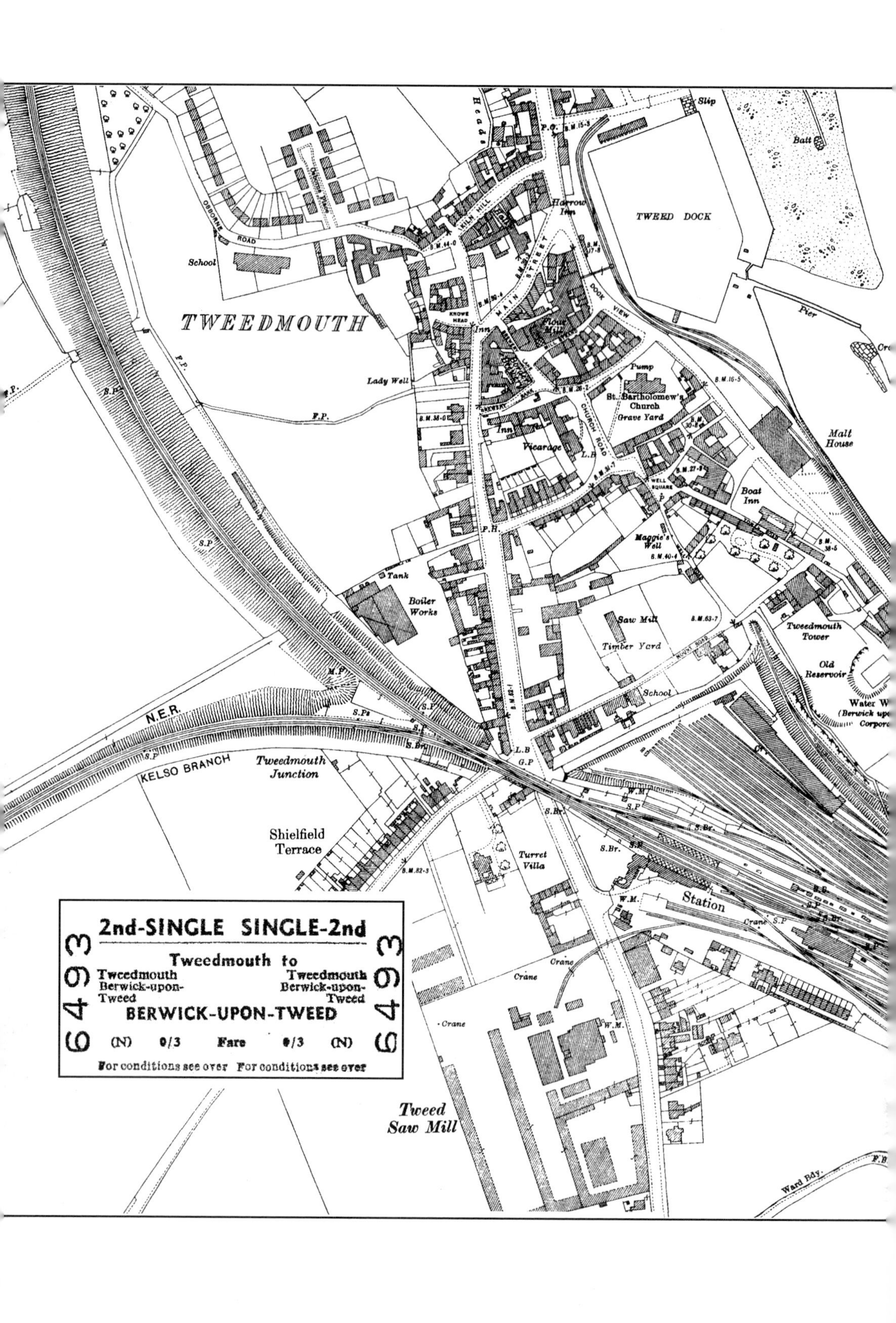

6493

2nd-SINGLE SINGLE-2nd

Tweedmouth to

Tweedmouth Berwick-upon-Tweed	Tweedmouth Berwick-upon-Tweed

BERWICK-UPON-TWEED

(N) 0/3 Fare 0/3 (N)

For conditions see over For conditions see over

6493

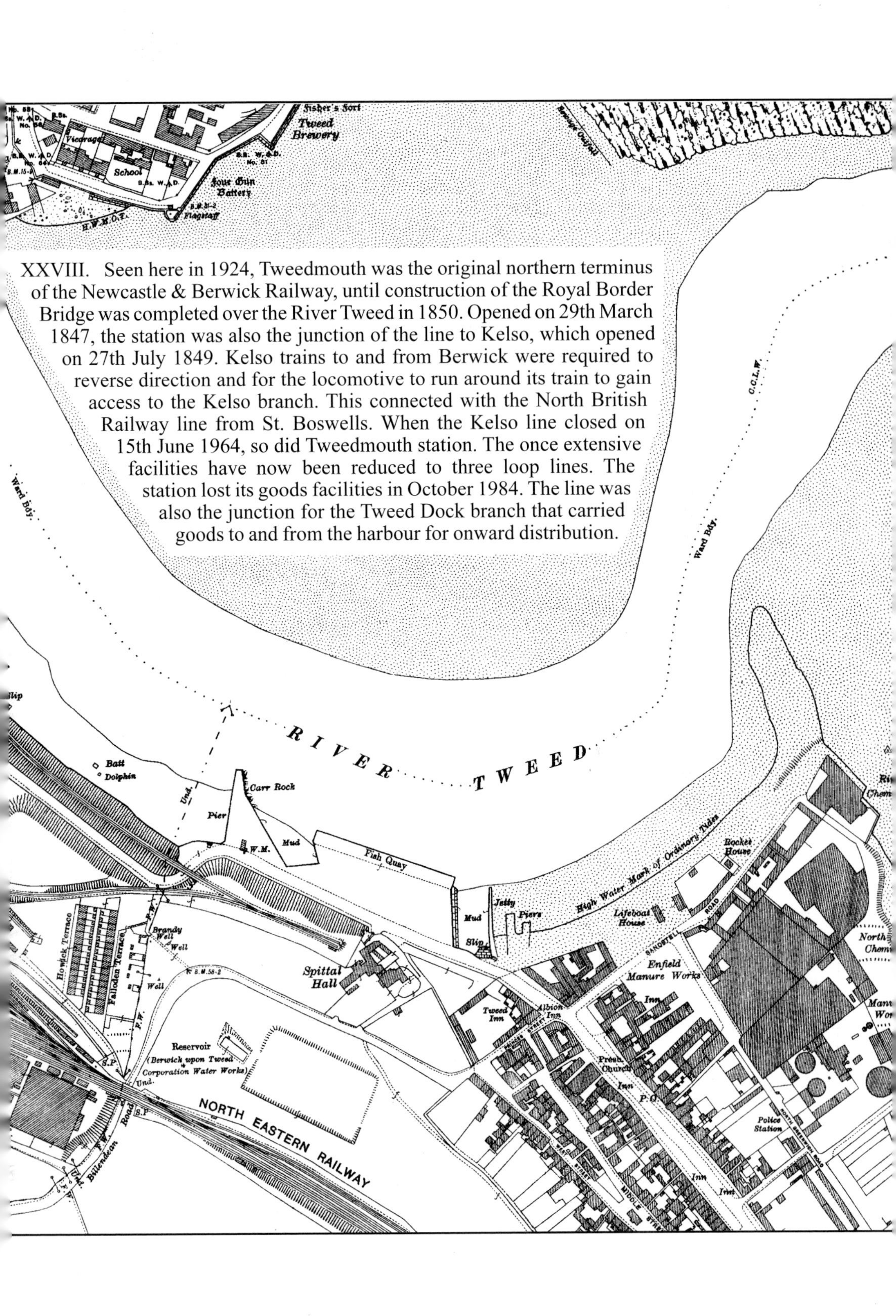

XXVIII. Seen here in 1924, Tweedmouth was the original northern terminus of the Newcastle & Berwick Railway, until construction of the Royal Border Bridge was completed over the River Tweed in 1850. Opened on 29th March 1847, the station was also the junction of the line to Kelso, which opened on 27th July 1849. Kelso trains to and from Berwick were required to reverse direction and for the locomotive to run around its train to gain access to the Kelso branch. This connected with the North British Railway line from St. Boswells. When the Kelso line closed on 15th June 1964, so did Tweedmouth station. The once extensive facilities have now been reduced to three loop lines. The station lost its goods facilities in October 1984. The line was also the junction for the Tweed Dock branch that carried goods to and from the harbour for onward distribution.

101. Here we have a photograph of the platform side on the same day. The Station Hotel and refreshment rooms were derelict. The NER proposed to close them in 1906 but the rooms were appreciated by the railwaymen and stayed in use until 1911. Efforts to find other uses continued over the years but ultimately failed and it was demolished with the station soon after Spring 1967. (J.C.Dean/NERA)

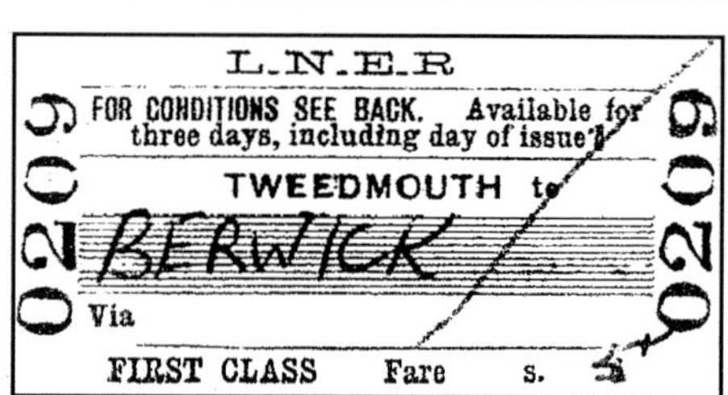

L.N.E.R
0209 FOR CONDITIONS SEE BACK. Available for three days, including day of issue 0209
TWEEDMOUTH to
BERWICK
Via
FIRST CLASS Fare s.

102. On 2nd July 1959 class V2 2-6-2 no 60913 was on an Up passenger train through the station. On the left, an unidentified A4 class 4-6-2 is making its way light engine to the shed. (Colour-Rail.com)

103. A class 37 Co-CoDE was in the goods yard as the photographer snapped it from an Up train entering the former Tweedmouth station site. The branch to Tweed Dock began from this goods yard with the first zigzag reversal in the north-east corner.
(W.Roberton)

Tweed Dock Branch

The Tweed Dock branch was goods only and was accessed from the goods yard, as seen on the last map. The building of the line was not without its challenges as Tweedmouth station lay on high ground, necessary for the Main Line to reach Berwick station on the north bank of the River Tweed, over the Royal Border Bridge. Construction of the dock line required it to zig-zag down to sea level and it opened only for goods traffic on 16th October 1878. For a train arriving from the north this resulted in two reversals: one to reach the yard and the second at the head shunt seen on the map just below the word 'River'. From there the line ran on an embankment adjacent to Spittal Road to descend to the dock itself. Amongst the traffic carried was grain, oil and timber.

104. The photographer was in the goods yard. The branch went under the wooden bridge to the next zig-zag where there were two stone viaducts. The line then reversed along Dock Road.
(J.C.Dean/NERA)

105. These are the viaducts on the zigzag. The rear viaduct has been demolished but the nearer one is still in place. The maximum train length down the line was four wagons, plus the locomotive because of the limited length of the zig-zag head shunts. The branch was worked by the Tweedmouth Yard pilot. This was an 0-6-0T from classes J77, J71 or J72. Latterly, it was worked by 0-6-0DM diesel shunters from classes 03 and 04. (Berwick Record Office)

106. Dock Road had the railway running alongside it but apart from a malt house, no industrial enterprise seemed to be large enough to merit a siding, and nor was there a goods shed. No business developed from Spittal, which would have required a siding to the south-east into the area of the original Spittal Railway. (Berwick Record Office)

107. Sailing vessels are moored inside the dock. When first built, there were lock gates to maintain the water in the dock. These were later removed, allowing larger vessels to enter but leaving the dock tidal. Tweed Dock can be seen top left on the last map (no. XXVIII). In 1872 The Harbour Commissioners gained an Act of Parliament to enable them to enlarge the facilities at Berwick. Improvements had already been carried out in 1808 but they were not sufficient to stop the loss of traffic to Leith and other east coast ports. The 1872 Act permitted the building of a large new dock and the construction of a railway, from Tweedmouth, in association with the NER to reach the new facility. Construction of the dock itself began in 1873. The line closed in around 1964. One of the viaducts and the railway embankment adjacent to the river were removed in 1975. (Berwick Record Office BRO 426-687)

108. The whole of the dock is visible in this aerial view, which includes the road bridges across the Tweed. The railway closed in 1964 and was removed shortly afterwards. The dock remains in commercial use today. (Berwick Record Office)

Ava Lodge
Spring
Vicarage
Gallows Knowe
Carlin Brae
Fishing Boat Depôt
Castle Bridge
Infant School
Auction Mart
Mary's Gate (Site of)
Castle Wall (Remains of)
Castle (Site of)
Station
Breakneck Stairs (Remains of)
Tunnel
Water Tower (Remains of)
White Wall (Remains of)
Castle Hotel
High Greens
Castle Vale
Tower (Remains of)
St. Mary's Church
School
Railway Street
P.O.
Inn
Castlegate
Gillie's Braes
Tweed House
New Road
Royal Border Bridge
Hang-a-dyke Neuk
High Water Mark of Ordinary Tides
Tweed Street
St. Mary's Convent
Scott's Place
School
Baptist Church
Ward Bdy.
River Tweed
North Eastern Railway
Tank
Tweedside Villa
Meg's Mount Bastion
Scotch Gate
Conqueror's Well
Boat Holes
Monument
Boat House
Lover's Walk
Blakewell Shad
Tweed Iron Works
Blakewell Road
Presb. Church
Manse
West End
Stone
Thatch House Tavern (P.H.)
Crane
Foundry
Pump
Yard Heads
Smithy
War Memorial
Fountain
Union Hotel
Berwick Bridge
English Gate (Site of)
Bailiff's Batt

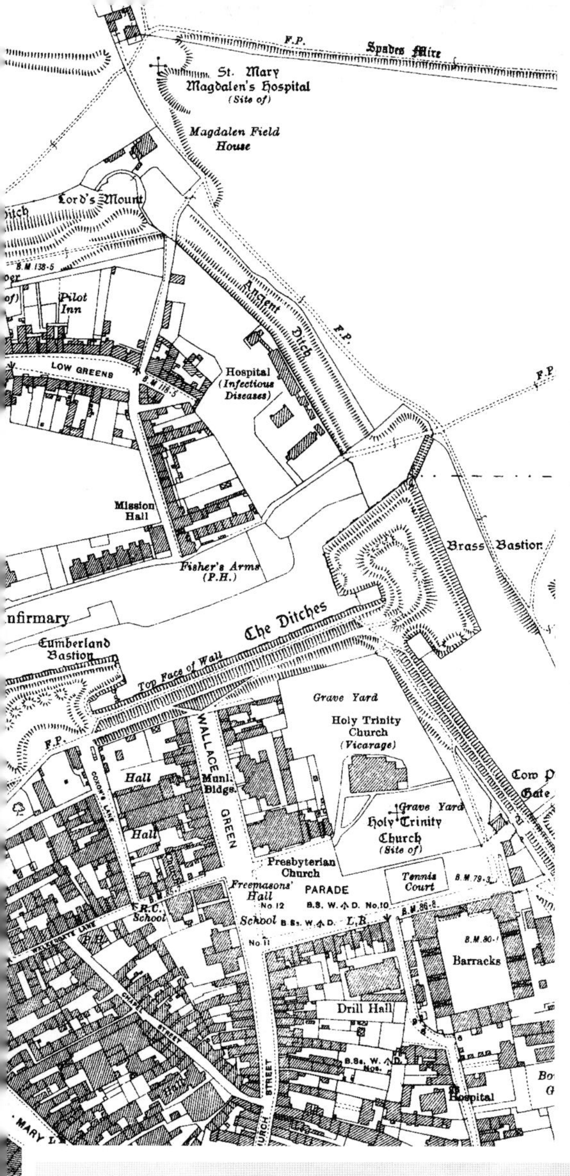

SOUTH OF BERWICK UPON TWEED

Royal Border Bridge

Prior to the completion of the 2162ft-long bridge, comprising of 28 60ft arches, Tweedmouth served as the terminus for three years, requiring passengers to transfer to horse-drawn carriages to cross the river by the 17th-century bridge. A temporary railway bridge, built mainly of timber, allowed trains to cross from the 10th October 1848.

← XXIX. This 1924 map shows the Royal Border Bridge, so named because in the past the River Tweed was the border between England and Scotland. Berwick was a Scottish Burgh until 1482, when it officially became part of England. In the preceding years, Berwick changed hands between Scotland and England 13 times! The current border is now 2½ miles north of the town. The opening of the Royal Border Bridge in 1850 completed the East Coast Main Line between England and Scotland. The former NBR terminus station on the north bank of the River was given two new through platforms, with the Newcastle & Berwick trains sharing the station in Berwick.

↓ 109. LNER Pacific no. 2568 *Sceptre* (later no. 60069) was crossing the bridge with a long Down train. The locomotive was a Gresley A1 class built by the North British Locomotive Co. in 1924 and rebuilt as a class A3 in May 1942. It was withdrawn in October 1962. (R.Humm coll.)

110. The steam crane has come out on to the bridge to do a little maintenance. In those days full protective clothing meant a jacket and a flat cap! This was the most popular vantage point for photographs, below the castle and looking south. (N. Forrest/Transport Treasury)

111. Class 40 1-Co-Co-1DE no. 40057 was hauling a loaded coal train north on the 30th January 1981. The famous signal gantry on the bridge has been replaced by a colour light signal. (B.Morrison)

↗ 112. The catenary for the electrification of the ECML was specially designed to be sympathetic to the Bridge. A CrossCountry franchise class 221 DMU was coming off the bridge into Berwick station on 24th June 2013. (D.A.Lovett)

Dewar's Granary Railway

Rails existed on the northern bank of the Tweed to transport grain from the granaries to the waiting ships. Grain is a major agricultural commodity in Northumberland and the nearby Scottish Borders. The rails were 18in gauge and were utilised by hand-pushed wagons conveying sacks from the granary reading for loading.

The granary was used by a Mr Dewar but the building, dating from the late 18th century, precedes him as Dewar began operations in the 19th century. The laying of the tracks also saw an arch cut through the historic town wall to aid operations.

The granary remained in use latterly as a grain and seed merchant's until the 1980s, after which it fell into ruin. The Grade II listed building was subsequently revitalised by the Berwick-upon-Tweed Preservation Trust and now houses a youth hostel, bistro and offices. During restoration, some rails were uncovered and have been left in situ. Information boards have been installed to tell the story of this rail-related site.

BERWICK upon TWEED

Map XXIX (on the previous pages) shows the station in 1924, prior to the rebuilding that was completed in 1927. The former NBR roundhouse engine shed is still standing; the facility was closed in 1924 by the London & North Eastern Railway which had assumed control of all railways in the Berwick area. Berwick's first station was opened on 22 June 1846 by the NBR, following completion of its line from Edinburgh. The Newcastle & Berwick Railway opened to Tweedmouth on 29th March 1847. The gap across the Tweed was finally closed by the building of the magnificent Royal Border Bridge. This opened in 1850 and from then on Berwick became the dominant station. To accommodate trains from Newcastle, two new through platforms were built alongside the former terminus station opening for traffic on 20th August 1850.

The more familiar 'upon-Tweed' was added to the station name on 1st January 1955. The station lost its goods facilities on 4th September 1967, with Tweedmouth continuing to serve the immediate area until October 1984 when it too lost its handling facilities, although a small yard is retained for engineering purposes. The original terminus station disappeared long ago, its foundations now being firmly underneath the current station car park.

113. NER 4-4-2 no. 730 was one of two locomotives designated by the LNER as class C8. Although Wilson Worsdell was CME he allowed his Chief Draughtsman, Walter M. Smith, to design locomotives as four cylinder compounds with Belpaire boilers, very different from Worsdell's own practices. No. 730 also had Stephenson motion. For all its life, from April 1906 to January 1935, it was used on ECML expresses including Royal workings. No wonder our elderly train spotters are looking over the fence. There appears to be a standard C7 Atlantic in the yard so maybe it was a trial. A G5 class 0-4-4T is on ECS on the extreme right. (ARPT)

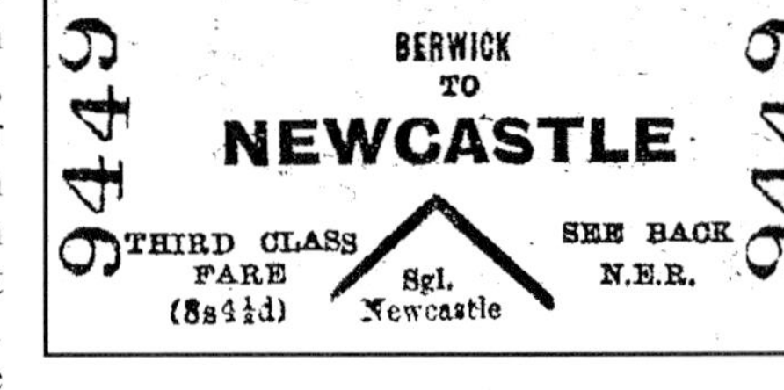

114. This was the exterior of the second station as it was in 1968. The first station was castellated as token reparation for ploughing the railway straight through a mediaeval castle! This was replaced in 1927. (J.C.Dean/NERA)

115. Amused and amusing passengers pose on 2nd June 1959. They are on the down side of the island platform. The lads' trousers are obviously the height of fashion. They are the BR West Hartlepool Goods Depot staff on an office day out. (R.F.Payne/ARPT)

116. A trackside view of the same platform has the lifts and the main office buildings on the right. (J.C.Dean/NERA)

117. Class A2/1 4-6-2 no. 60509 *Waverley* has the signal to take the Up 'Talisman' out of the station and on to the bridge. Built in November 1944, *Waverley* was withdrawn in August 1960. (N.E.Stead/Transport Library)

118. This is the same end of the station, on 21st July 1964, but with a platform-based view of class A3 4-6-2 no. 60080 *Dick Turpin*, which was fitted with German-style smoke deflectors on November 1961. It was withdrawn in October 1964 so has only four months left in action. (N.E.Stead/Transport Library)

119. The prototype High Speed Train enters the station going south. No. 41001 was leading and 41002 is the subject of the photographer. This was a wrong-line working as the track was under repair in the Up platform. Note that the metal sign for 'Berwick' is still on the bankside. (J.C.Dean/NERA)

120. We finish our trip with a more modern form of permanent way machine in DR 72201.This was Plasser & Theurer Dynamic Track Stabiliser model 62-N seen here in August 1989. Behind it is part of the Berwick Castle wall that survived the Railway's onslaught! (D.A.Lovett)

Further pictures of Berwick-upon-Tweed appear in the following albums: *Berwick to Drem*, *Berwick to St. Boswells via Kelso* **and** *St. Boswells to Berwick via Duns*.

Easebourne Midhurst GU29 9AZ. Tel:01730 813169

A-978 0 906520 B- 978 1 873793 C- 978 1 901706 D-978 1 904474
E - 978 1 906008 F - 978 1 908174 G - 978 1 910356

Our RAILWAY titles are listed below. Please check availability by looking at our website www.middletonpress.co.uk, telephoning us or by requesting a Brochure which includes our LATEST RAILWAY TITLES also our TRAMWAY, TROLLEYBUS, MILITARY and COASTAL series.

email:info@middletonpress.co.uk

A
Abergavenny to Merthyr C 91 8
Abertillery & Ebbw Vale Lines D 84 5
Aberystwyth to Carmarthen E 90 1
Allhallows - Branch Line to A 62 8
Alnmouth to Berwick G 50 0
Alton - Branch Lines to A 11 6
Ambergate to Buxton G 28 9
Ambergate to Mansfield G 39 5
Andover to Southampton A 82 6
Ascot - Branch Lines around A 64 2
Ashburton - Branch Line to B 95 4
Ashford - Steam to Eurostar B 67 1
Ashford to Dover A 48 2
Austrian Narrow Gauge D 04 3
Avonmouth - BL around D 42 5
Aylesbury to Rugby D 91 3

B
Baker Street to Uxbridge D 90 6
Bala to Llandudno E 87 1
Banbury to Birmingham D 27 2
Banbury to Cheltenham E 63 5
Bangor to Holyhead F 01 7
Bangor to Portmadoc E 72 7
Barking to Southend C 80 2
Barmouth to Pwllheli E 53 6
Barry - Branch Lines around D 50 0
Bartlow - Branch Lines to F 27 7
Basingstoke to Salisbury A 89 4
Bath Green Park to Bristol C 36 9
Bath to Evercreech Junction A 60 4
Beamish 40 years on rails E94 9
Bedford to Wellingborough D 31 9
Berwick to Drem F 64 2
Berwick to St. Boswells F 75 8
B'ham to Tamworth & Nuneaton F 63 5
Birkenhead to West Kirby F 61 1
Birmingham to Wolverhampton E253
Blackburn to Hellifield F 95 6
Bletchley to Cambridge D 94 4
Bletchley to Rugby E 07 9
Bodmin - Branch Lines around B 83 1
Boston to Lincoln F 80 2
Bournemouth to Evercreech Jn A 46 8
Bournemouth to Weymouth A 57 4
Bradshaw's History F18 5
Bradshaw's Rail Times 1850 F 13 0
Branch Lines series - see town names
Brecon to Neath D 43 2
Brecon to Newport D 16 6
Brecon to Newtown E 06 2
Brighton to Eastbourne A 16 1
Brighton to Worthing A 03 1
Bristol to Taunton D 03 6
Bromley South to Rochester B 23 7
Bromsgrove to Birmingham D 87 6
Bromsgrove to Gloucester D 73 9
Broxbourne to Cambridge F16 1
Brunel - A railtour D 74 6
Bude - Branch Line to B 29 9
Burnham to Evercreech Jn B 68 0
Buxton to Stockport G 32 6

C
Cambridge to Ely D 55 5
Canterbury - BLs around B 58 9
Cardiff to Dowlais (Cae Harris) E 47 5
Cardiff to Pontypridd E 95 6
Cardiff to Swansea E 42 0
Carlisle to Hawick E 85 7
Carmarthen to Fishguard E 66 6
Caterham & Tattenham Corner B251
Central & Southern Spain NG E 91 8
Chard and Yeovil - BLs a C 30 7
Charing Cross to Dartford A 75 8
Charing Cross to Orpington A 96 3
Cheddar - Branch Line to B 90 9
Cheltenham to Andover C 43 7
Cheltenham to Redditch D 81 4
Chesterfield to Lincoln G 21 0
Chester to Birkenhead F 21 5
Chester to Manchester F 51 2
Chester to Rhyl E 93 2
Chester to Warrington F 40 6
Chichester to Portsmouth A 14 7
Clacton and Walton - BLs to F 04 8
Clapham Jn to Beckenham Jn B 36 7
Cleobury Mortimer - BLs a E 18 5
Clevedon & Portishead - BLs to D180
Consett to South Shields E 57 4
Cornwall Narrow Gauge D 56 2
Corris and Vale of Rheidol E 65 9
Coventry to Leicester G 00 5
Craven Arms to Llandeilo E 35 2
Craven Arms to Wellington E 33 8
Crawley to Littlehampton A 34 5
Crewe to Manchester F 57 4
Crewe to Wigan G 12 8
Cromer - Branch Lines around C 26 0
Cromford and High Peak G 35 7
Croydon to East Grinstead B 48 0
Crystal Palace & Catford Loop B 87 1
Cyprus Narrow Gauge E 13 0

D
Darjeeling Revisited F 09 3
Darlington Leamside Newcastle E 28 4
Darlington to Newcastle D 98 2
Dartford to Sittingbourne B 34 3
Denbigh - Branch Lines around F 32 1
Derby to Chesterfield G 11 1
Derby to Nottingham G 45 6
Derby to Stoke-on-Trent F 93 2
Derwent Valley - BL to the D 06 7
Devon Narrow Gauge E 09 3
Didcot to Banbury D 02 9
Didcot to Swindon C 84 0
Didcot to Winchester C 13 0
Diss to Norwich G 22 7
Dorset & Somerset NG D 76 0
Douglas - Laxey - Ramsey E 75 8
Douglas to Peel C 88 8
Douglas to Port Erin C 55 0
Douglas to Ramsey D 39 5
Dover to Ramsgate A 78 9
Drem to Edinburgh G 06 7
Dublin Northwards in 1950s E 31 4
Dunstable - Branch Lines to E 27 7

E
Ealing to Slough C 42 0
Eastbourne to Hastings A 27 7
East Cornwall Mineral Railways D 22 7
East Croydon to Three Bridges A 53 6
Eastern Spain Narrow Gauge E 56 7
East Grinstead - BLs to A 07 9
East Kent Light Railway A 61 1
East London - Branch Lines of C 44 4
East London Line B 80 0
East of Norwich - Branch Lines E 69 7
Effingham Junction - BLs a A 74 1
Ely to Norwich C 90 1
Enfield Town & Palace Gates D 32 6
Epsom to Horsham A 30 7
Eritrean Narrow Gauge E 38 3
Euston to Harrow & Wealdstone C 89 5
Exeter to Barnstaple B 15 2
Exeter to Newton Abbot C 49 9
Exeter to Tavistock B 69 5
Exmouth - Branch Lines to B 00 8

F
Fairford - Branch Line to A 52 9
Falmouth, Helston & St. Ives C 74 1
Fareham to Salisbury A 67 3
Faversham to Dover B 05 3
Felixstowe & Aldeburgh - BL to D 20 3
Fenchurch Street to Barking C 20 8
Festiniog - 50 yrs of enterprise C 83 3
Festiniog 1946-55 E 01 7
Festiniog in the Fifties B 68 8
Festiniog in the Sixties B 91 6
Ffestiniog in Colour 1955-82 F 25 3
Finsbury Park to Alexandra Pal C 02 8
French Metre Gauge Survivors F 88 8
Frome to Bristol B 77 0

G
Gainsborough to Sheffield G 17 3
Galashiels to Edinburgh F 52 9
Gloucester to Bristol D 35 7
Gloucester to Cardiff D 66 1
Gosport - Branch Lines around A 36 9
Greece Narrow Gauge D 72 2
Guildford to Redhill A 63 5

H
Hampshire Narrow Gauge D 36 4
Harrow to Watford D 14 2
Harwich & Hadleigh - BLs to F 02 4
Harz Revisited F 62 8
Hastings to Ashford A 37 6
Hawick to Galashiels F 36 9
Hawkhurst - Branch Line to A 66 6
Hayling - Branch Line to A 12 3
Hay-on-Wye - BL around D 92 0
Haywards Heath to Seaford A 28 4
Hemel Hempstead - BLs to D 88 3
Henley, Windsor & Marlow - BLa C77 2
Hereford to Newport D 54 8
Hertford & Hatfield - BLs a E 58 1
Hertford Loop E 71 0
Hexham to Carlisle D 75 3
Hexham to Hawick F 08 6
Hitchin to Peterborough D 07 4
Holborn Viaduct to Lewisham A 81 9
Horsham - Branch Lines to A 02 4
Hull, Hornsea and Withernsea G 27 2
Huntingdon - Branch Line to A 93 2

I
Ilford to Shenfield C 97 0
Ilfracombe - Branch Line to B 21 3
Ilkeston to Chesterfield G 26 5
Ipswich to Diss F 81 9
Ipswich to Saxmundham C 41 3
Isle of Man Railway Journey F 94 9
Isle of Wight Lines - 50 yrs C 12 3
Italy Narrow Gauge F 17 8

K
Kent Narrow Gauge C 45 1
Kettering to Nottingham F 82-6
Kidderminster to Shrewsbury E 10 9
Kingsbridge - Branch Line to C 98 7
Kings Cross to Potters Bar E 62 8
King's Lynn to Hunstanton F 58 1
Kingston & Hounslow Loops A 83 3
Kingswear - Branch Line to C 17 8

L
Lambourn - Branch Line to C 70 3
Launceston & Princetown - BLs C 19 2
Leeds to Selby G 47 0
Leek - Branch Line From G 01 2
Leicester to Burton F 85 7
Leicester to Nottingham G 15 9
Lewisham to Dartford A 92 5
Lincoln to Cleethorpes F 56 7
Lincoln to Doncaster G 03 6
Lines around Stamford F 98 7
Lines around Wimbledon B 75 6
Lines North of Stoke G 29 6
Liverpool Street to Chingford D 01 2
Liverpool Street to Ilford C 34 5
Llandeilo to Swansea E 46 8
London Bridge to Addiscombe B 20 6
London Bridge to East Croydon A 58 1
Longmoor - Branch Lines to A 41 3
Looe - Branch Line to C 22 2
Loughborough to Ilkeston G 24 1
Loughborough to Nottingham F 68 0
Lowestoft - BLs around E 40 6
Ludlow to Hereford E 14 7
Lydney - Branch Lines around E 26 0
Lyme Regis - Branch Line to A 45 1
Lynton - Branch Line to B 04 6

M
Machynlleth to Barmouth E 54 3
Maesteg and Tondu Lines F 06 2
Majorca & Corsica Narrow Gauge F 41 3
Manchester to Bacup G 46 3
Mansfield to Doncaster G 23 4
March - Branch Lines around B 09 1
Market Drayton - BLs around F 67 3
Market Harborough to Newark F 86 4
Marylebone to Rickmansworth D 49 4
Melton Constable to Yarmouth Bch E031
Midhurst - Branch Lines of E 78 9
Midhurst - Branch Lines to F 00 0
Minehead - Branch Line to A 80 2
Mitcham Junction Lines B 01 5
Monmouth - Branch Lines to E 20 8
Monmouthshire Eastern Valleys D 71 5
Moretonhampstead - BL to C 27 7
Moreton-in-Marsh to Worcester D 26 5
Morpeth to Bellingham F 87 1
Mountain Ash to Neath D 80 7

N
Newark to Doncaster F 78 9
Newbury to Westbury C 66 6
Newcastle to Alnmouth G 36 4
Newcastle to Hexham D 69 2
New Mills to Sheffield G 44 9
Newport (IOW) - Branch Lines to A 26 0
Newquay - Branch Lines to C 71 0
Newton Abbot to Plymouth C 60 4
Newtown to Aberystwyth E 41 3
Northampton to Peterborough F 92 5
North East German NG D 44 9
Northern Alpine Narrow Gauge F 37 6
Northern France Narrow Gauge C 75 8
Northern Spain Narrow Gauge E 83 3
North London Line B 94 7
North of Birmingham F 55 0
North of Grimsby - Branch Lines G 09 8
North Woolwich - BLs around C 65 9
Nottingham to Boston F 70 3
Nottingham to Kirkby Bentinck G 38 8
Nottingham to Lincoln F 43 7
Nottingham to Mansfield G 52 4
Nuneaton to Loughborough G 08 1

O
Ongar - Branch Line to E 05 5
Orpington to Tonbridge B 03 9
Oswestry - Branch Lines around E 60 4
Oswestry to Whitchurch E 81 9
Oxford to Bletchley D 57 9
Oxford to Moreton-in-Marsh D 15 9

P
Paddington to Ealing C 37 6
Paddington to Princes Risborough C819
Padstow - Branch Line to B 54 1
Peebles Loop G 19 7
Pembroke and Cardigan - BLs to F 29 1
Peterborough to Kings Lynn E 32 1
Peterborough to Lincoln F 89 5
Peterborough to Newark F 72 7
Plymouth - BLs around B 98 5
Plymouth to St. Austell C 63 5
Pontypool to Mountain Ash D 65 4
Pontypridd to Merthyr F 14 7
Pontypridd to Port Talbot E 86 4
Porthmadog 1954-94 - BLa B 31 2
Portmadoc 1923-46 - BLa B 13 8
Portsmouth to Southampton A 31 4
Portugal Narrow Gauge E 67 3
Potters Bar to Cambridge D 70 8
Preston to Blackpool G 16 6
Princes Risborough - BL to D 05 0
Princes Risborough to Banbury C 85 7

R
Railways to Victory C 16 1
Reading to Basingstoke B 27 5
Reading to Didcot C 79 6
Reading to Guildford A 47 5
Redhill to Ashford A 73 4
Return to Blaenau 1970-82 C 64 2
Rhyl to Bangor F 15 4
Rhymney & New Tredegar Lines E 48 2
Rickmansworth to Aylesbury D 61 6
Romania & Bulgaria NG E 23 9
Romneyrail C 32 1
Ross-on-Wye - BLs around E 30 7
Ruabon to Barmouth E 84 0
Rugby to Birmingham E 37 6
Rugby to Loughborough F 12 3
Rugby to Stafford F 07 9
Rugeley to Stoke-on-Trent F 90 1
Ryde to Ventnor A 19 2

S
Salisbury to Westbury B 39 8
Salisbury to Yeovil B 06 0
Sardinia and Sicily Narrow Gauge F 50 5
Saxmundham to Yarmouth C 69 7
Saxony & Baltic Germany Revisited F 71 0
Saxony Narrow Gauge D 47 0
Scunthorpe to Doncaster G 34 0
Seaton & Sidmouth - BLs to A 95 6
Selsey - Branch Line to A 04 8
Sheerness - Branch Line to B 16 2
Sheffield towards Manchester G 18 0
Shenfield to Ipswich E 96 3
Shrewsbury - Branch Line to A 86 4
Shrewsbury to Chester E 70 3
Shrewsbury to Crewe F 48 2
Shrewsbury to Ludlow E 21 5
Shrewsbury to Newtown E 29 1
Sirhowy Valley Line E 12 3
Sittingbourne to Ramsgate A 90 1
Skegness & Mablethorpe - BL to F 84 0
Slough to Newbury C 56 7
South African Two-foot gauge E 51 2
Southampton to Bournemouth A 42 0
Southend & Southminster BLs E 76 5
Southern Alpine Narrow Gauge F 22 2
Southern France Narrow Gauge C 47 5
South London Line B 46 6
South Lynn to Norwich City F (
Southwold - Branch Line to A
Spalding - Branch Lines aroun
Spalding to Grimsby F 65 9 6
Stafford to Chester F 34 5
Stafford to Wellington F 59 8
St Albans to Bedford D 08 1
St. Austell to Penzance C 67 3
St. Boswell to Berwick F 44 4
Steaming Through Isle of Wigh
Stourbridge to Wolverhampton
St. Pancras to Barking D 68 5
St. Pancras to Folkestone E 88
St. Pancras to St. Albans C 78
Stratford to Cheshunt F 53 6
Stratford-u-Avon to Birminghar
Stratford-u-Avon to Cheltenhar
Sudbury - Branch Lines to F 1
Surrey Narrow Gauge C 87 1
Sussex Narrow Gauge C 68 0
Swaffham - Branch Lines arou
Swanage to 1999 - BL to A 33
Swanley to Ashford B 45 9
Swansea - Branch Lines arour
Swansea to Carmarthen E 59
Swindon to Bristol C 96 3
Swindon to Gloucester D 46 3
Swindon to Newport D 30 2
Swiss Narrow Gauge C 94 9

T
Talyllyn 60 E 98 7
Tamworth to Derby F 76 5
Taunton to Barnstaple B 60 2
Taunton to Exeter C 82 6
Taunton to Minehead F 39 0
Tavistock to Plymouth B 88 6
Tenterden - Branch Line to A 2
Three Bridges to Brighton A 35
Tilbury Loop C 86 4
Tiverton - BLs around C 62 8
Tivetshall to Beccles D 41 8
Tonbridge to Hastings A 44 4
Torrington - Branch Lines to B
Tourist Railways of France G 0
Towcester - BLs around E 39
Tunbridge Wells BLs A 32 1

U
Upwell - Branch Line to B 64 0
Uttoxeter to Macclesfield G 05
Uttoxetor to Buxton G 33 3

V
Victoria to Bromley South A 98
Victoria to East Croydon A 40
Vivarais Revisited E 08 6

W
Walsall Routes F 45 1
Wantage - Branch Line to D 2
Wareham to Swanage 50 yrs
Waterloo to Windsor A 54 3
Waterloo to Woking A 38 3
Watford to Leighton Buzzard D
Wellingborough to Leicester F
Welshpool to Llanfair E 49 9
Wenford Bridge to Fowey C 0
Westbury to Bath B 55 8
Westbury to Taunton C 76 5
West Cornwall Mineral Rlys D
West Croydon to Epsom B 08
West German Narrow Gauge
West London - BLs of C 50 5
West London Line B 84 8
West Wiltshire - BLs of D 12 8
Weymouth - BLs A 65 9
Willesden Jn to Richmond B 7
Wimbledon to Beckenham C
Wimbledon to Epsom B 62 6
Wimborne - BLs around A 97
Wirksworth - Branch Lines to
Wisbech - BLs around C 01 7
Witham & Kelvedon - BLs a E
Woking to Alton A 59 8
Woking to Portsmouth A 25 3
Woking to Southampton A 55
Wolverhampton to Shrewsbur
Wolverhampton to Stafford F
Worcester to Birmingham D 9
Worcester to Hereford D 38 8
Worthing to Chichester A 06
Wrexham to New Brighton F
Wroxham - BLs around F 31

Y
Yeovil - 50 yrs change C 38 3
Yeovil to Dorchester A 76 5
Yeovil to Exeter A 91 8
York to Scarborough F 23 9